¿Amazing English! ™

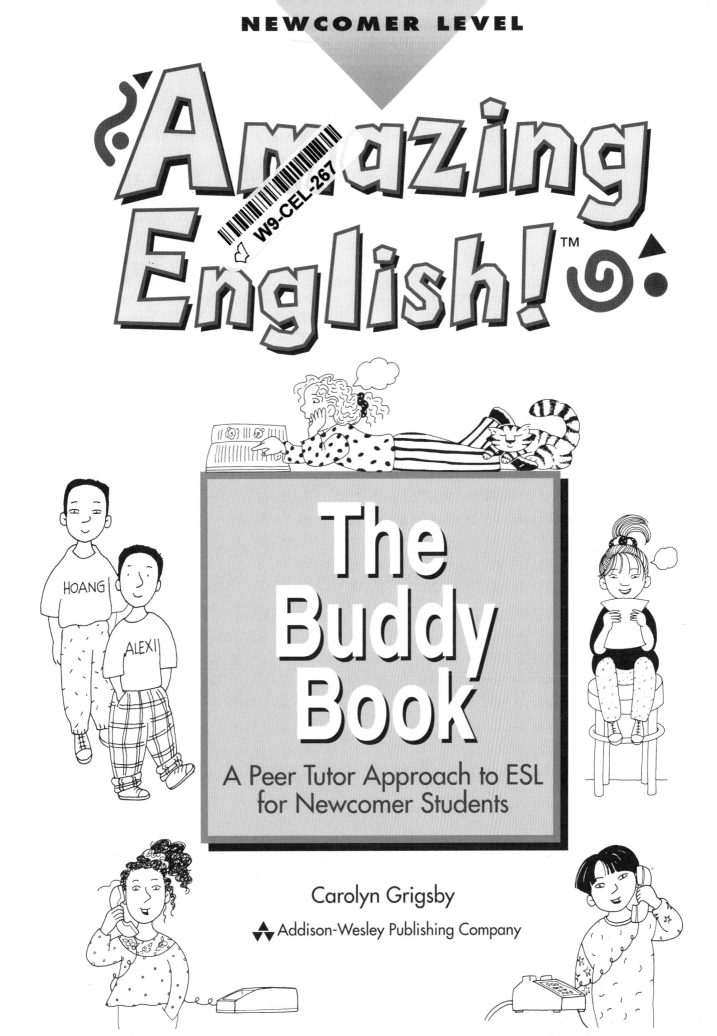

The Buddy Book

A Peer Tutor Approach to ESL for Newcomer Students

Carolyn Grigsby

▲ Addison-Wesley Publishing Company

A Publication of the World Language Division

Acknowledgments

Many thanks to the friends and colleagues who have contributed to the creation of this book.

I am grateful to Paula Harrington, Ella Baff, and Kristin Shepherd for their encouragement and advice on all aspects of this project.

Special thanks also go to Betsy Morris and John Helyer for invaluable insights; to Esther Guerrero, Jill Korengold, Lydia Zele, and Alison Date for professional opinions and feedback; to Jose Nieto and the Jefferson School District for supporting me as a mentor teacher in ESL; to my fellow MATEFL students at San Francisco State for their enthusiasm and support; and an extra special thanks to Maria Luisa Cabrera and Wendy Walker for sharing their expertise and time.

I also want to express my appreciation to Elinor Chamas, Judith Bittinger, and Peggy Alper at Addison-Wesley for their editorial guidance and assistance.

Finally, thanks to my family for their love and encouragement.

Director of Product Development: Judith Bittinger

Executive Editor: Elinor Chamas

Editorial Development: Judith Bittinger, Peggy T. Alper

Cover and Text Design: Taurins Design Associates

Production and Manufacturing: James W. Gibbons

Illustrators: Delores Bego 10; Susan Miller 9, 13, 14, 65, 67, 68, 72, 73, 76, 78, 97, 99, 100, 103, 104, 107, 108, 110; Chris Reed 11, 17, 18, 19, 21, 35, 36, 37, 38, 51, 54, 55, 56, 57, 59, 60, 64, 69, 74, 80, 83, 86, 89, 90, 91, 92, 94, 95, 98, 101.

Black line masters may be copied for classroom use.

ISBN 0-201-85387-6
8 9 10 11 12 13 14 15 CRS 0807060504030201

CONTENTS

Talking About Food and Family

Describing Locations and Actions

Describing Abilities/Schedules

Buddy Book Certificate

INSIDE THE GRADE-LEVEL CLASSROOM

This book is part of the AMAZING ENGLISH Program. The activities are designed for newcomer English-language learners in the upper elementary grades (3rd-6th). With your supervision, a native-English-speaking student—a Buddy Tutor—will help the Buddy Learner.

CHOOSING BUDDY TUTORS

Peer tutors. Peer tutors need not be the "best" students in your class, but they should be fluent speakers of English. Choose students who you think can make newcomers feel at ease.

It is also not important for peer tutors to speak the native languages of the newcomers. In fact, it is probably better if they don't. If you have students who can translate for the newcomers, use them to help with content areas, such as social studies, science, and mathematics.

You can also rotate Buddies as you feel it's appropriate. You may want to use a different student every day, or you may want to use the same student for several days. It's better not to rely on one student to be the only Buddy. That student might miss too much of his or her own work or grow tired of the Buddy role.

TRAINING BUDDIES

If you will be using a variety of students as Buddies, it's a good idea to begin with a class introduction to the Buddy system.

Buddy Tutor instructions. Read "To the Buddy Tutor," on page 8, together with your entire class. Then brainstorm ideas and discuss these questions:

▷ What is it like to move to a new country?

▷ What is it like to learn a new language?

▷ How should Buddies act (what should they do, and what should they say)?

Model for your students the right and wrong way to be a Buddy. Focus especially on how to help someone without doing the work for them. Stress using positive, encouraging words. You may also want to introduce a simple reward system to encourage students to become good Buddies.

There are various book-making projects included in *The Buddy Book.* Model making the books for your students.

USING BUDDY BOOK ACTIVITIES

The Buddy Book instructions are written simply, and the activities are not difficult. They are designed to help the newcomer acquire basic English vocabulary quickly and in a holistic context. Buddy Learners will work at different paces and levels of interest. Don't rush them. Most of the early activities in the book are designed for students who come from a non-Roman-alphabet literacy background (Chinese, Arabic, Greek, etc.) or for students who are not literate in their own languages.

Black line masters. This book consists of reproducible black line masters, so you can decide in advance which pages to copy and distribute to Buddy pairs. (For example, you will want to copy the page titled

"To the Buddy Tutor" for each student who becomes a Tutor.) There is no need to have Buddies cover the material in the order in which it appears here. The needs of Buddy Learners will vary—some may not need to learn to write letters and numbers, for example. Reproduce and distribute the pages that are most appropriate for *your* students.

Buddy symbols. A Buddy Tutor symbol and a Buddy Learner symbol appear with the instructions, so students will always know which instructions apply to them. For the majority of activities, the Buddy Tutor is a helper; the Buddy Learner is responsible for accomplishing the tasks. In some cases, however, you may find it useful to have the Buddies work on a project as a team (e.g., when they make a school schedule or a mini-book).

Ways to use *The Buddy Book.* This book is extremely flexible and adaptable to your classroom schedule. It can be used in any of these ways:

▷ as a language arts activity for one or two hours of the day;

▷ as a basics/survival curriculum for newcomers' first few weeks;

▷ as a free-time enrichment activity;

▷ as a resource for homework assignments.

You can decide how best to integrate the newcomer into your classroom. Subjects like math, art, and physical education are easiest for the newcomer. In social studies and science, incorporate newcomers by choosing activities that are simple and easy for them to succeed in—for example, drawing pictures; choosing

a few key vocabulary words to look up in their language; making maps; or participating in science experiments. (See Staff Development and Related Resources, on page 7.)

Each page in this book has a separate activity that builds on the previous activity. There are often suggestions for extensions at the bottom of the page. These can also be used for homework. The newcomer will need lots of practice with new words and phrases. Each exercise can be repeated a number of times. When appropriate, send the Learner's work home (**Home-School Connection**). Invite the Learner's family to comment on these pages. Choose some activities as examples of language acquisition, and save the relevant pages in the Learner's **Assessment Portfolio.**

Monitor the Buddy Tutor to make sure he or she is working *with* the Buddy Learner and not doing the work *for* the newcomer. Also, discuss every activity with the Buddy Tutor before he or she pairs off with the Buddy Learner to make sure the Tutor understands the tasks.

Materials needed. You'll need to provide the following materials for Buddy Tutors and Buddy Learners:

▷ lined paper

▷ colored construction paper

▷ white drawing paper

▷ crayons

▷ pencils

▷ glue

▷ scissors

▷ catalogs and magazines

▷ a picture dictionary

If possible, set up a Buddy Learning Center in your classroom, where these materials are readily available.

Placement test. When a newcomer has completed all the activities in *The Buddy Book*, use the AMAZING ENGLISH Placement Test to determine which level of the program may be appropriate to the student's level of language ability. It will probably be Level B or C. Don't forget, however, that the older newcomer has missed extensive literature and language experiences in Levels K, A, and B. Don't hesitate to use more Big Books, activities, or songs than are in *The Buddy Book*—especially if the newcomer doesn't seem quite ready for the full AMAZING ENGLISH curriculum. (See Staff Development and Related Resources, below.)

OUTSIDE THE GRADE-LEVEL CLASSROOM

These activities can also be used for a self-contained newcomer class or for a pull-out ESL class. In either setting, the teacher can be the Buddy and can model the activities on the board for the students.

In a newcomer class, you can begin doing these activities with the entire class. Later in the year, when most students have progressed beyond the beginning activities, the more "advanced" students can be Buddies to any new students that come in. An alternative is to invite native-English-speaking Buddies from a grade-level classroom to help in the ESL setting. This is a good way to socialize the newcomers.

BENEFITS OF THE BUDDY SYSTEM

▷ Students are eager to be "teachers" and show their mastery of skills and expertise. Being a Buddy Tutor increases their confidence and self-esteem.

▷ Almost any student can be a Buddy. By choosing Buddies who are not necessarily the highest academic achievers, you can raise *their* self-esteem and confidence as well.

▷ Language and social skills developed in the classroom while working on these activities will extend to the playground. These new skills will help newcomer students to make friends more easily and to integrate more smoothly into the classroom.

▷ Most of the activities in this book provide opportunities for cultural sharing between the Buddy Learner and the Buddy Tutor. Take advantage of this for the entire classroom environment.

STAFF DEVELOPMENT

See *The Amazing How-To Handbook, The Art of Teaching ESL* video and *The Art of Teaching The Natural Approach* video for ideas and information.

RELATED RESOURCES

See *The Addison-Wesley Picture Dictionary, Alligator at the Airport,* and the *Amazing Video Libraries.* These resources will be especially useful for students working on the alphabet, picture-word correspondences, vocabulary development, and listening skills.

Hi! You are going to be helping a new student in your class learn English. Your teacher can help you and answer questions, but you can do most of this by yourself.

Before you start, imagine that you moved to a new country and were starting a new school. No one speaks your language and you don't understand what the teacher says to you. You can't ask anyone for help, because you don't know how to ask. You don't even know which bathroom to use, since you don't know how they write **boys** or **girls** in this new language. You know you're just as smart as any of these other kids, but all you can do is point and smile.

If you can imagine a little bit of this, you're going to be a great Buddy Tutor! Buddy Learners (the newcomers) are a lot like you are—they just don't know the same words you do . . . not yet. But watch—with your help they'll be speaking English fast.

Work with your Buddy on all the Buddy Study activities. There will be instructions for you to read on each page. Look at the top of the page for the symbols and .

Your symbol is . It will tell you what you are to do in the activity.

The symbol for the newcomer is . It will tell what he or she should be doing. It's a good idea to read both instructions out loud, so that the newcomer can start learning to understand directions in English.

Remember, you are *helping* a new student to do these activities. *Don't do them **for** the newcomer.* Sometimes the newcomer will draw pictures of words, and you will write the word for him or her in English. Other times you may need to do one or two examples to show the new student what to do. Sometimes you can get your Buddy started and then go back to your own work. There are also projects you can work together on. If you have a question, ask your teacher.

HAVE FUN!

What's Your Name?

Point to the words and say them. Write your name. Have your Buddy do the same.

Listen, look, and write.

Hi. My name is

_____.

What's your name?

_____ is my first name.

_____ is my last name.

My name is

_____.

_____ is **my** first name.

_____ is **my** last name.

GETTING STARTED ● Understanding and responding to questions; practicing the order of names in English; practicing rhythm, stress, and intonation in dialogues. You might want to do the first few pages with the Buddies to be sure they understand the system. Although Learners practice writing the English alphabet on pages 21-33, they can learn to write their names beforehand. After Buddies write their names, they can practice the "dialogue"; note that the Buddy Learner should emphasize the word *my*.

Where Are You From?

Say the words and fill in the blank.

Listen, say, and write.

I'm from _____.

Where are you from?

I'm from _____.

Find your country and color it. Help your Buddy do the same.

Listen and draw.

GETTING STARTED ● Home-school connection; mapping; world geography; exchanging personal information; developing cross-cultural appreciation. Buddy Tutors can help Learners write the names of their countries here; they will actually practice writing the letters of the English alphabet on pages 21-33. Other students in the class might want to share information about where they, their parents, grandparents, or other family members are from. Have students take this page home to share with their families.

Show your Buddy how to ask classmates, "What's your first name?" and "What's your last name?" Classmates will sign their own names.

Ask and listen.

FIRST NAME	LAST NAME
1.	
2.	
3.	
4.	
5.	
6.	
7.	
8.	
9.	
10.	

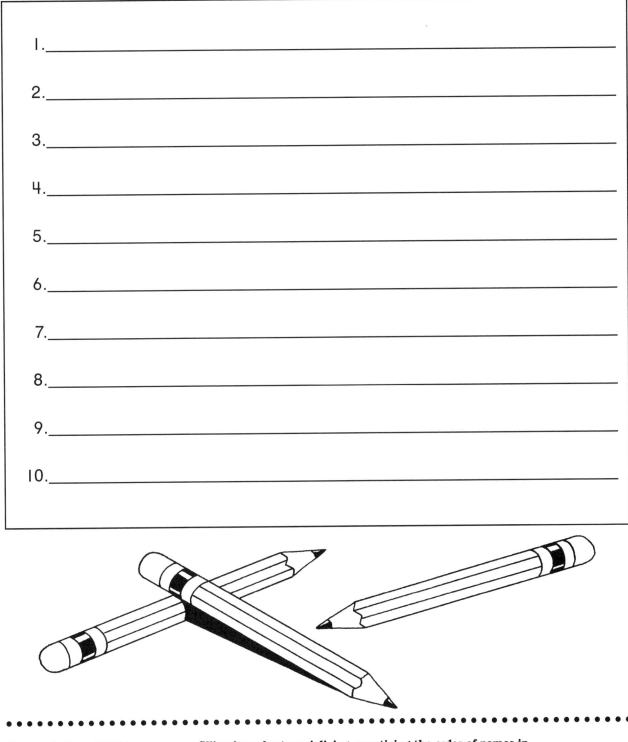

GETTING STARTED ● Taking a survey; filling in a chart; socializing; practicing the order of names in English. You may want to set aside a special time for this activity; or, you may want to allow Buddies to interrupt other students briefly during quiet study time.

Work with your Buddy to fill in this checklist.

Listen and say.

DOES YOUR BUDDY...

☐ have textbooks?

☐ have help to cover textbooks (and know which books can be written in)?

☐ have pencil, crayons, a ruler, and scissors (or know where to get them when needed)?

☐ know which supplies and books may go home?

☐ know where and when to sharpen pencils?

☐ know where and how to line up (before school, at recess, for lunch)?

☐ know where the bathrooms are?

☐ know where the water fountain is?

☐ know the lunch procedures (where to buy food, where to sit, when to leave for the playground)?

☐ know the school schedule (when school begins and ends, times for recesses and lunch, etc.)?

☐ understand classroom rules?

☐ understand playground and general school rules?

☐ know the teacher's name and the classroom number?

GETTING STARTED ● Getting along in school; listening comprehension; following directions; organizational planning; vocabulary development. Model for Buddy Tutor how to use gestures and objects (e.g., school supplies) if Learner doesn't understand a question. Take Buddies on a school tour. Name rooms, school items, rules, and routines. Don't expect Buddy Tutors to check off all the entries here after only one tour or explanation. They can return to page as appropriate.

Classroom Instructions

Read all the classroom instructions out loud as you point to the pictures.

Look and listen.

1. Please sit down.

2. Please get in line.

3. Please go to the board.

4. Please work with your Buddy.

5. Please open your books.

6. Please look at the board.

GETTING STARTED ● Listening comprehension; using illustrations to gain understanding; following directions (TPR). Have the Buddy Tutor "drill" the Buddy Learner in following these directions if that is appropriate for the students and your classroom situation.

Asking Permission

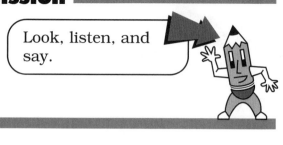

Teach your Buddy how to ask permission. Don't worry if your Buddy doesn't get all the words right at first. Come back every few days to pages 13 and 14 to remind your Buddy about classroom language.

Look, listen, and say.

1. May I sharpen my pencil?

2. May I go to the bathroom?

3. May I get a drink?

4. May I go to the nurse?

5. May I listen to the tape?

6. May I work at the computer?

© Addison-Wesley Publishing Company

GETTING STARTED ● Listening comprehension; reading comprehension; practicing rhythm, stress, and intonation in dialogues; using illustrations to gain understanding. Have Buddies take turns being Teacher and answering the questions ("Yes, you may"; "No, not right now," etc.) so they can role-play dialogues in context.

Point to each number and say it. Count the shapes. Have your Buddy repeat.

Listen, look, and say.

0

1 △

2 ○ ○

3 □ □ □

4 ▭ ▭ ▭ ▭

5 △ △ △ △ △

6 ○ ○ ○ ○ ○ ○

7 □ □ □ □ □ □ □

8 ▭ ▭ ▭ ▭ ▭ ▭ ▭ ▭

9 □ □ □ □ □ □ □ □

10 △ △ △ △ △ △ △ △ △ △

LEARNING NUMBERS AND LETTERS ● Identifying numbers and shapes (geometry). If Buddy Learner is ready, present vocabulary in print: *triangles, circles, squares,* and *rectangles.* Refer to this page when Buddies work on shapes, on pages 53-57.

Writing Numbers

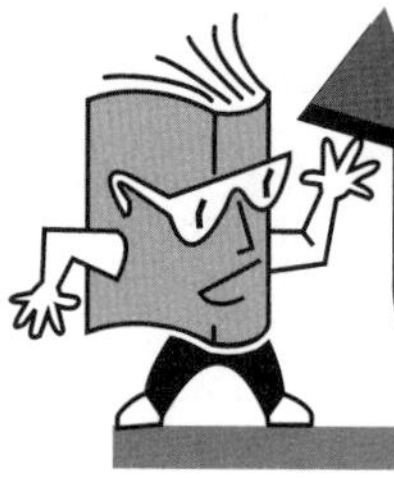

Read each number out loud. Then help your Buddy write the numbers.

Listen and write.

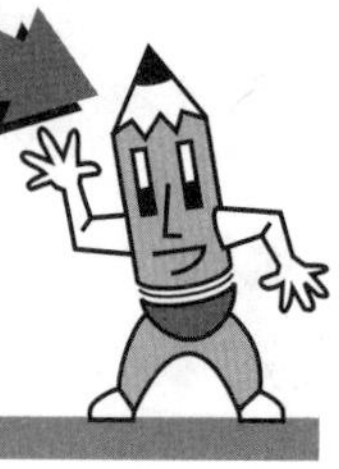

1 1

2 2

3 3

4 4

5 5

6 6

7 7

8 8

9 9

10 10

Learning Numbers and Letters ● **Writing mechanics: practicing writing numbers; listening comprehension; identifying numbers; sequencing.** Encourage Buddy Tutor to get Buddy Learner started and then leave Learner alone to complete page. You may want to check Learner's work.

What's Your Telephone Number?

Fill in your telephone number. Help your Buddy do the same.

Listen and write.

My telephone number is

_____.

My telephone number is

_____.

Now make a Buddy Study Phone Number book. Cut a piece of 8 1/2 x 11 inch paper in half. Fold and staple the pieces. Ask your teacher for help if you need it. Now ask for the names and phone numbers of friends in your class. Decorate the cover.

Ask and write.

LEARNING NUMBERS AND LETTERS ● Listening comprehension; following directions; hands-on project; socializing. If necessary, help Buddies make their Buddy Study phone books. You may want to suggest they make two books, one for the Buddy Tutor, one for the Buddy Learner. Buddies can take turns asking classmates for phone numbers, which they then write in their respective phone books. You may want to save this page in the Learner's **Assessment Portfolio.**

Numbers 11-20

Point to each number and say it. Count the objects and say what they are. Have your Buddy repeat. Don't worry if your Buddy can't pronounce all the words correctly. Return to this page for practice.

Listen, look, and say.

11

12

13

14

15

16

17

18

19

20

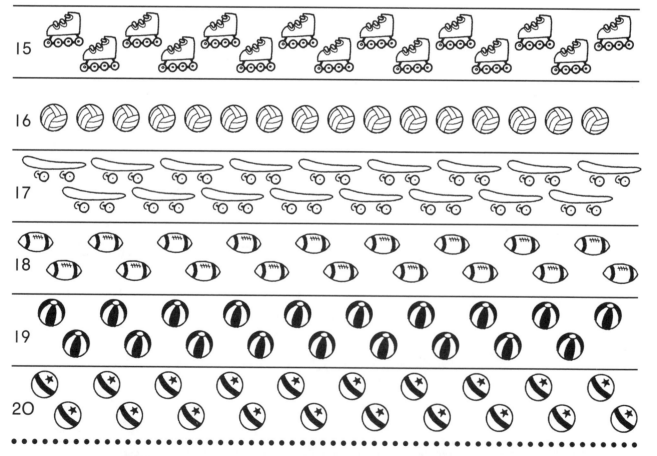

© Addison-Wesley Publishing Company

LEARNING NUMBERS AND LETTERS ● Identifying numbers; counting; vocabulary development. Emphasize to Tutor that the point here is learning numbers 11-20. The names of the objects should be considered passive vocabulary.

18

What Time Is It?

A. Cut out the clock hands. Attach them to the clock with a brad. Show and say each time (1-12) on the hour ("It's _____ o'clock"). Have your Buddy repeat.

Listen, look, and say.

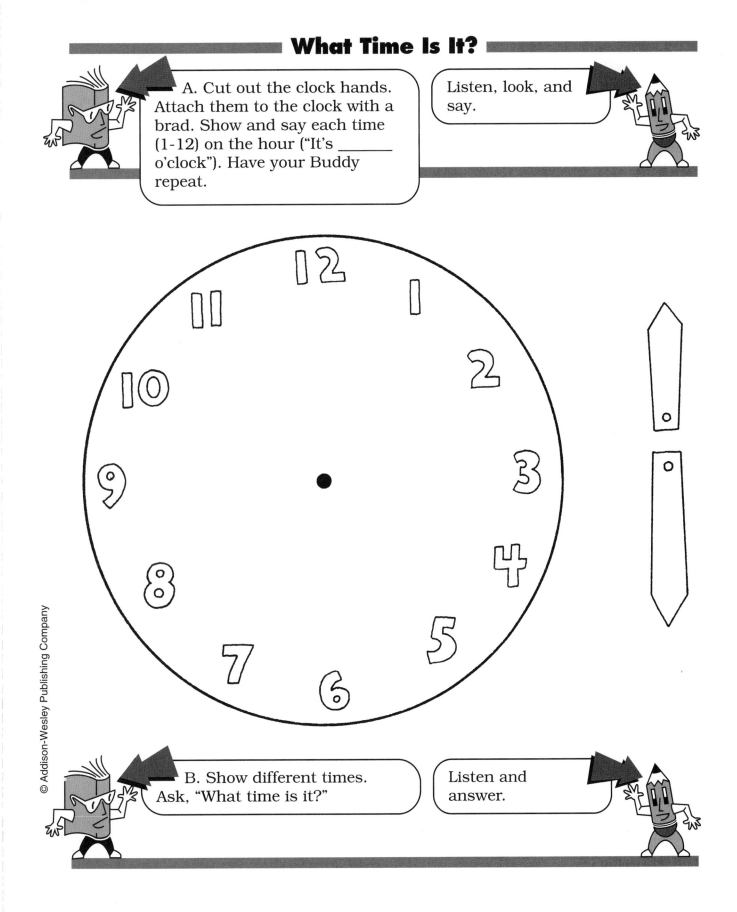

B. Show different times. Ask, "What time is it?"

Listen and answer.

LEARNING NUMBERS AND LETTERS ● **Telling time; practicing numbers; asking for/giving information.** If time on the half hour is important to your school day, have Tutor teach now. For part B, Learner answers with contraction: "It's_____o'clock." Encourage Buddies to switch roles so Learner can ask "What time is it?" and manipulate clock hands. Extension: If appropriate for Buddies and your classroom situation, encourage discussion about what happens at specific times during the school day.

The Alphabet

Read every letter. Have your Buddy repeat. Then point to letters out of order. Have your Buddy tell you what they are.

Listen, look, and say.

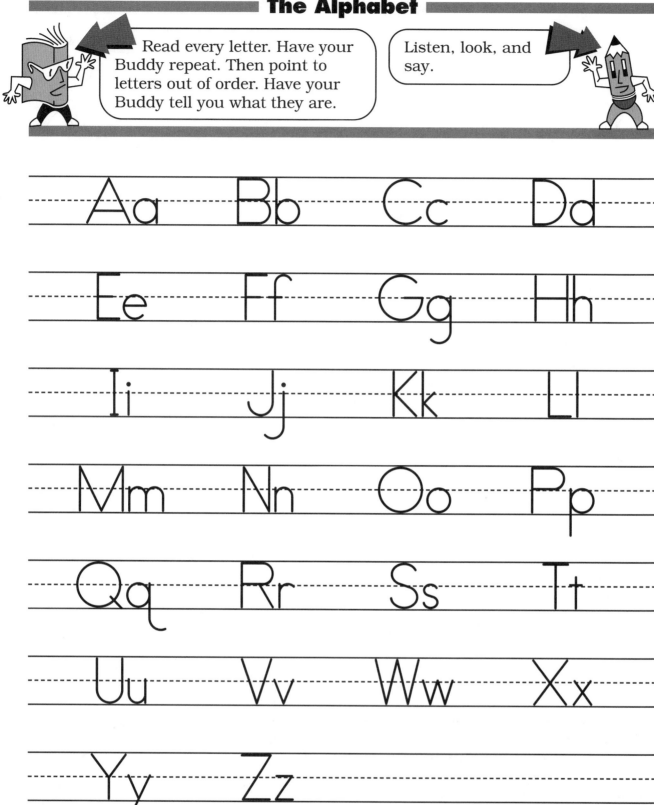

Aa Bb Cc Dd

Ee Ff Gg Hh

Ii Jj Kk Ll

Mm Nn Oo Pp

Qq Rr Ss Tt

Uu Vv Ww Xx

Yy Zz

LEARNING NUMBERS AND LETTERS ● Identifying letters; reciting the alphabet. Encourage Buddies to spend as much time as necessary on this page. This is especially important for Buddy Learners whose first languages are written in non-Roman alphabets.

Help your Buddy write letters and words.

Write the letters and the words.

A

a

a

ant

apple

B

B

b

b

boy

book

LEARNING NUMBERS AND LETTERS ● Identifying the letters of the alphabet; writing words; art. For pages 21-33, encourage Buddy Learners to make a personal word book. They can use *The Addison-Wesley Picture Dictionary* and *Alligator at the Airport* to find pictures of words to draw and label.

21

The Alphabet

Write the letters and the words.

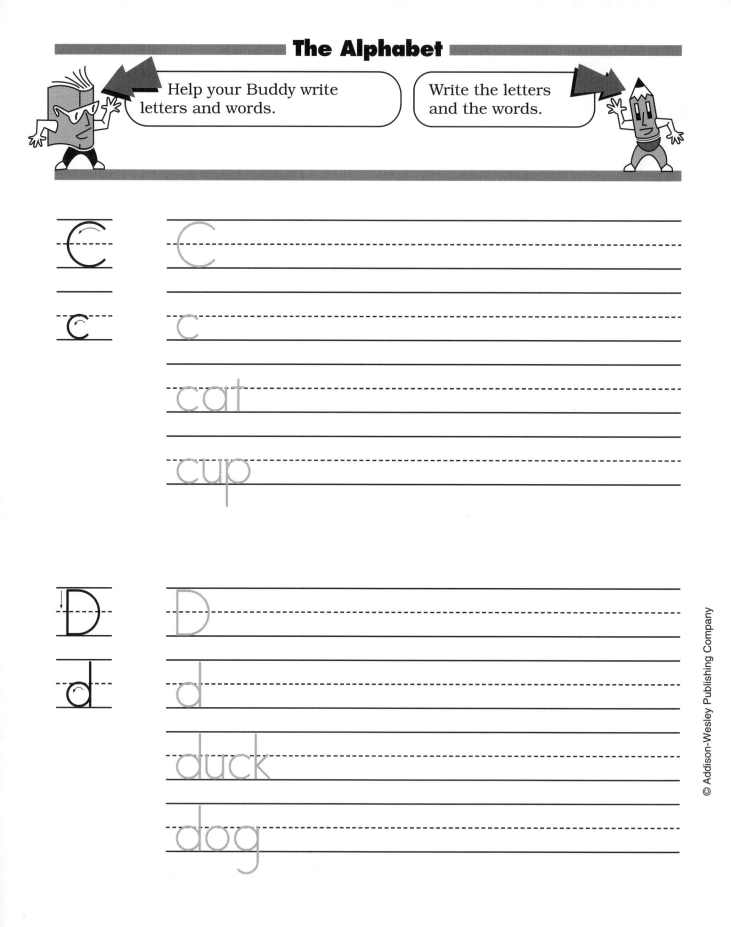

C

c

c

c

cat

cup

D

d

D

d

duck

dog

Help your Buddy write letters and words.

Write the letters and the words.

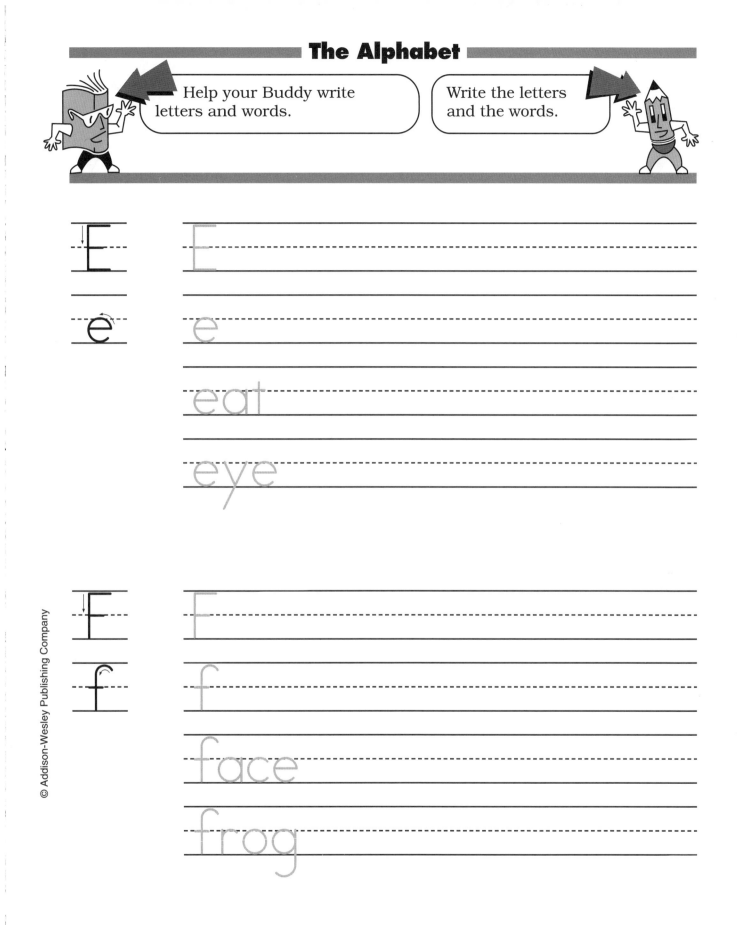

E

e

eat

eye

F

f

face

frog

The Alphabet

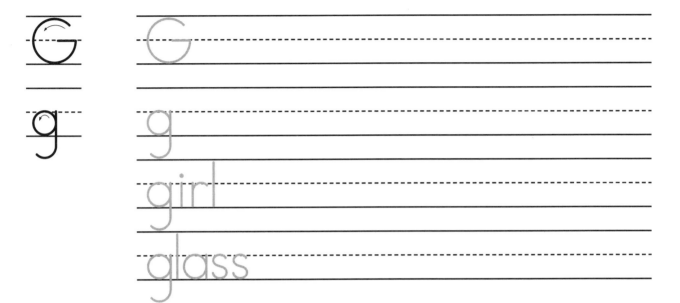

G G

g g
girl
glass

H H
h h
hat
house

Help your Buddy write letters and words.

Write the letters and the words.

I

i

ice

in

J

j

jump

job

Help your Buddy write letters and words.

Write the letters and the words.

K

k

kite

key

L

l

light

leaf

Help your Buddy write letters and words.

Write the letters and the words.

M
M

m
m

me

map

N
N

n
n

nose

neck

The Alphabet

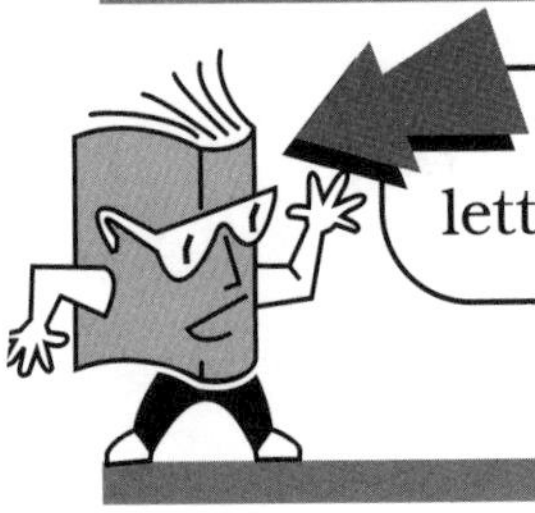

O O

o o

one

orange

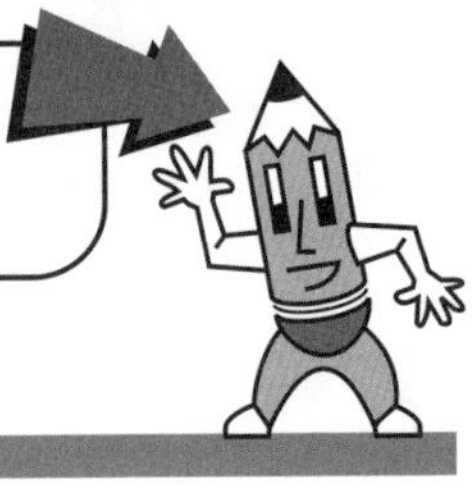

P P

p p

pencil

pig

Help your Buddy write letters and words.

Write the letters and the words.

Q

q

q

quiz

queen

R

R

r

r

rain

robot

Help your Buddy write letters and words.

Write the letters and the words.

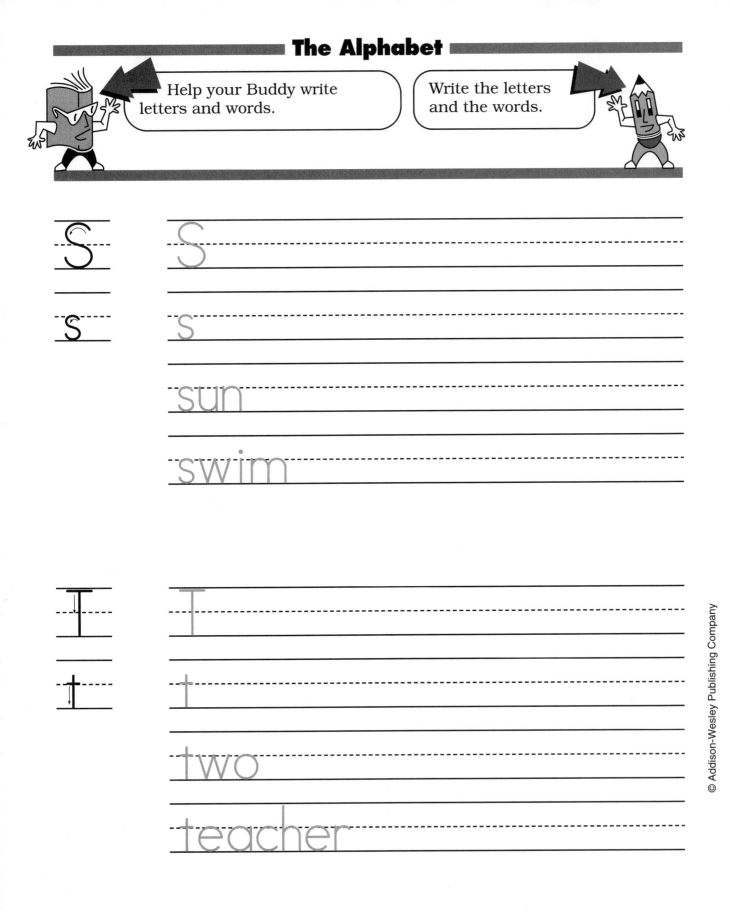

S

s

S

s

sun

swim

T

t

T

t

two

teacher

The Alphabet

Help your Buddy write letters and words.

Write the letters and the words.

U u

U

u

us

umbrella

V v

V

v

van

vest

The Alphabet

Help your Buddy write letters and words.

Write the letters and the words.

W
w

W
w
whale
women

X
x

X
x
x-ray

LEARNING NUMBERS AND LETTERS

Help your Buddy write letters and words.

Write the letters and the words.

Y Y

y y

you

yes

Z Z

Z z

zoo

zebra

AMAZING WORDS

Help your Buddy write alphabet words from the alphabet pages you worked on. The words can be any ones your Buddy wants. One word goes in each square. Fill up the grid. Then take turns choosing squares. Read the words. Try to read 3 in a row correctly to get the bonus points. The player with the most points wins.

Write, say, and win!

3 in a row = 10 Bonus Points

Each square = 5 points

© Addison-Wesley Publishing Company

LEARNING NUMBERS AND LETTERS ● Playing a game; socializing; practicing word recognition. This game is played like Tic-Tac-Toe. Copy this page before it is filled in so that Buddies can play more than once. If you have more than one Buddy Learner in your class, they can exchange gameboards and play against one another. To make rules more challenging: use each word in a sentence, name another word that begins (ends) with the same letter, etc. Buddies can "handicap" the Tutor with harder rules. Players can cover their squares with a coin or button.

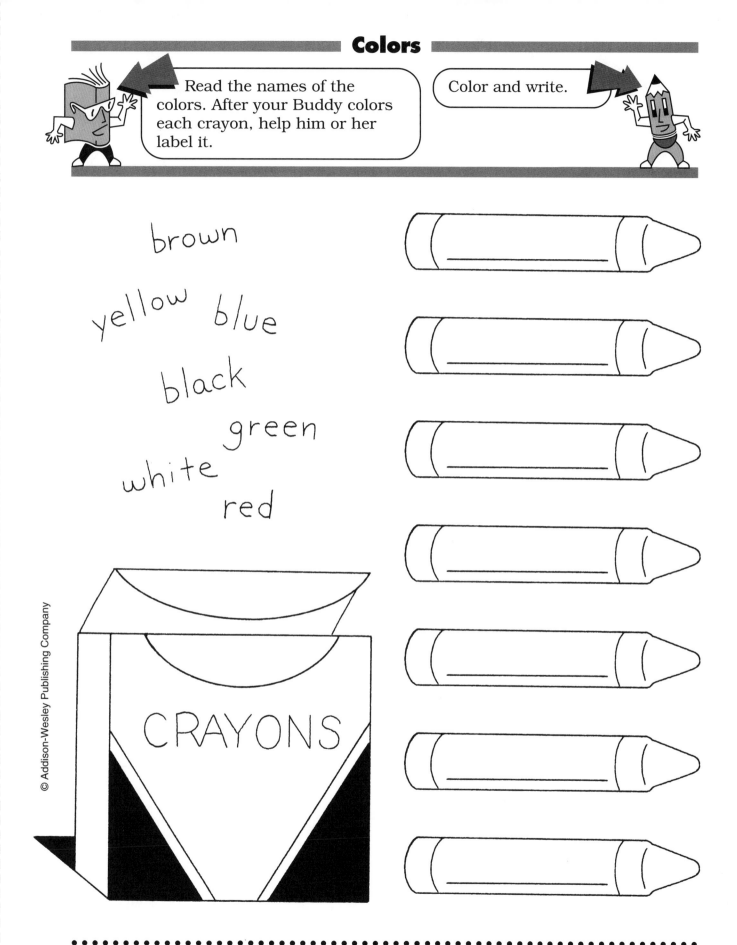

Read the names of the colors. After your Buddy colors each crayon, help him or her label it.

Color and write.

brown

yellow blue

black

green

white

red

CRAYONS

LEARNING COLORS AND SHAPES ● Identifying colors; hands-on activity; writing color names. Buddy Learners should color each crayon, using the color names given. Be sure Buddy Tutor instructs Learner to write the names of the colors on the crayons. If necessary for clarity, Buddies can write the color name above or below each crayon instead.

Read the directions below to your Buddy. Help him or her find each object.

Listen and color.

Color the apple red.
Color the paper white.
Color the books green.
Color the pen black.
Color the desk brown.

Color the chalk yellow.
Color the pencils brown.
Color the ruler blue.
Color the plant green.
Color the glue white.

LEARNING COLORS AND SHAPES ● Following directions; hands-on activity; identifying colors and classroom objects. This page provides a useful introduction to classroom vocabulary. You may want to save this page in the Learner's Assessment Portfolio.

36

Help your Buddy find and name things that are blue. Label each drawing and say the words out loud.

Say, draw, and write.

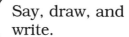

bird

eyes

© Addison-Wesley Publishing Company

LEARNING COLORS AND SHAPES ● **Identifying objects and colors; hands-on activity; vocabulary development; writing.** Let Buddies look through *The* Addison-Wesley *Picture Dictionary* and books and magazines for vocabulary. Assist with labeling if necessary.

Help your Buddy choose words to draw and write on the lines. Read all the sentences together.

Draw and write.

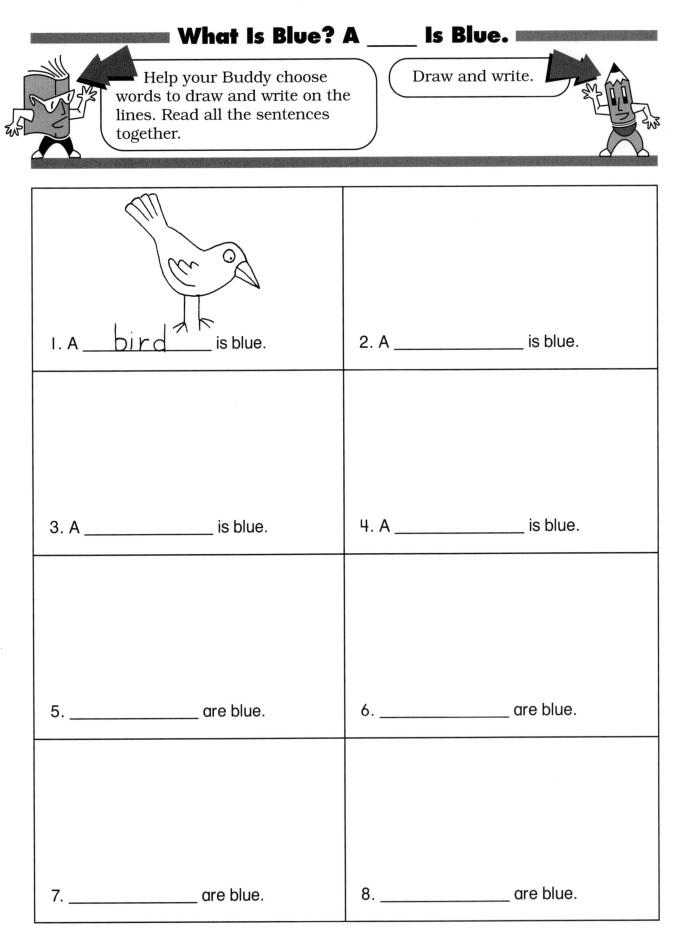

1. A ___bird___ is blue.

2. A _____ is blue.

3. A _____ is blue.

4. A _____ is blue.

5. _____ are blue.

6. _____ are blue.

7. _____ are blue.

8. _____ are blue.

LEARNING COLORS AND SHAPES ● Identifying colors and objects; hands-on activity; vocabulary development; reading sentences. Use *The Addison-Wesley Picture Dictionary*, picture books, and magazines. Be sure Buddy Tutor knows that first four nouns are to be singular, last four plural. Have Buddies write more sentences on a separate piece of paper if they need more practice. Encourage Tutors to use the same sentence pattern for more colors.

What Is Red?

Help your Buddy find and name things that are red. Label each drawing and say the words out loud.

Say, draw, and write.

LEARNING COLORS AND SHAPES ● Identifying objects and colors; hands-on activity; vocabulary development; writing. Let Buddies look through *The Addison-Wesley Picture Dictionary* and books and magazines for vocabulary. Assist with labeling if necessary.

Help your Buddy choose words to draw and write on the lines. Read all the sentences together.

Draw and write.

1. A _____ is red.

2. A _____ is red.

3. A _____ is red.

4. A _____ is red.

5. _____ are red.

6. _____ are red.

7. _____ are red.

8. _____ are red.

LEARNING COLORS AND SHAPES ● Identifying colors and objects; hands-on activity; vocabulary development; reading sentences. Use *The Addison Wesley Picture Dictionary*, picture books, and magazines. Be sure Buddy Tutor knows that first four nouns are to be singular, last four plural. Use of *is/are*, like *he/she*, is just something Learner must memorize, so don't worry if Learner mixes them up early on. Have Buddies write more sentences on a separate piece of paper if they need more practice.

Help your Buddy find and name things that are yellow. Label each drawing and say the words out loud.

Say, draw, and write.

LEARNING COLORS AND SHAPES ● **Identifying objects and colors; hands-on activity; vocabulary development; writing.** Let Buddies look through *The Addison-Wesley Picture Dictionary* and books and magazines for vocabulary. Assist with labeling if necessary.

Help your Buddy choose words to draw and write on the lines. Read all the sentences together.

Draw and write.

1. A _____ is yellow.

2. A _____ is yellow.

3. A _____ is yellow.

4. A _____ is yellow.

5. _____ are yellow.

6. _____ are yellow.

7. _____ are yellow.

8. _____ are yellow.

LEARNING COLORS AND SHAPES ● Identifying colors and objects; hands-on activity; vocabulary development; reading sentences. Use *The Addison-Wesley Picture Dictionary*, picture books, and magazines. Be sure Buddy Tutor knows that first four nouns are to be singular, last four plural. Use of *is/are*, like *he/she*, is just something Learner must memorize, so don't worry if Learner mixes them up early on. Have Buddies write more sentences on a separate piece of paper if they need more practice.

42

What Is Green?

Help your Buddy find and name things that are green. Label each drawing and say the words out loud.

Say, draw, and write.

LEARNING COLORS AND SHAPES ● Identifying objects and colors; hands-on activity; vocabulary development; writing. Let Buddies look through the *The Addison-Wesley Picture Dictionary* and books and magazines for vocabulary. Assist with labeling if necessary.

43

Help your Buddy choose words to draw and write on the lines. Read all the sentences together.

Draw and write.

1. A _____ is green.

2. A _____ is green.

3. A _____ is green.

4. A _____ is green.

5. _____ are green.

6. _____ are green.

7. _____ are green.

8. _____ are green.

LEARNING COLORS AND SHAPES ● Identifying colors and objects; hands-on activity; vocabulary development; reading sentences. Use *The Addison-Wesley Picture Dictionary*, picture books, and magazines. Be sure Buddy Tutor knows that first four nouns are to be singular, last four plural. Use of *is/are*, like *he/she*, is just something Learner must memorize, so don't worry if Learner mixes them up early on. Have Buddies write more sentences on a separate piece of paper if they need more practice.

Help your Buddy find and name things that are brown. Label each drawing and say the words out loud.

Say, draw, and write.

LEARNING COLORS AND SHAPES ● Identifying objects and colors; hands-on activity; vocabulary development; writing. Let Buddies look through the *The Addison-Wesley Picture Dictionary* and books and magazines for vocabulary. Assist with labeling if necessary.

45

What Is Brown? A _____ Is Brown.

Help your Buddy choose words to draw and write on the lines. Read all the sentences together.

Draw and write.

1. A _____ is brown.

2. A _____ is brown.

3. A _____ is brown.

4. A _____ is brown.

5. _____ are brown.

6. _____ are brown.

7. _____ are brown.

8. _____ are brown.

© Addison-Wesley Publishing Company

LEARNING COLORS AND SHAPES ● Identifying colors and objects; hands-on activity; vocabulary development; reading sentences. Use *The Addison-Wesley Picture Dictionary*, picture books, and magazines. Be sure Buddy Tutor knows that first four nouns are to be singular, last flour plural. Use of *is/are*, like *he/she*, is just something Learner must memorize, so don't worry if Learner mixes them up early on. Have Buddies write more sentences on a separate piece of paper if they need more practice.

Help your Buddy find and name things that are black. Label each drawing and say the words out loud.

Say, draw, and write.

LEARNING COLORS AND SHAPES ● **Identifying objects and colors; hands-on activity; vocabulary development; writing.** Let Buddies look through the *The Addison-Wesley Picture Dictionary* and books and magazines for vocabulary. Assist with labeling if necessary.

47

Help your Buddy choose words to draw and write on the lines. Read all the sentences together.

Draw and write.

1. A _____ is black.

2. A _____ is black.

3. A _____ is black.

4. A _____ is black.

5. _____ are black.

6. _____ are black.

7. _____ are black.

8. _____ are black.

LEARNING COLORS AND SHAPES ● Identifying colors and objects; hands-on activity; vocabulary development; reading sentences. Use *The Addison-Wesley Picture Dictionary*, picture books, and magazines. Be sure Buddy Tutor knows that first four nouns are to be singular, last flour plural. Use of is/are, like *he/she*, is just something Learner must memorize, so don't worry if Learner mixes them up early on. Have Buddies write more sentences on a separate piece of paper if they need more practice.

What Is White?

Help your Buddy find and name things that are white. Label each drawing and say the words out loud.

Say, draw, and write.

© Addison-Wesley Publishing Company

LEARNING COLORS AND SHAPES ● Identifying objects and colors; hands-on activity; vocabulary development; writing. Let Buddies look through the *The Addison-Wesley Picture Dictionary* and books and magazines for vocabulary. Assist with labeling if necessary.

Help your Buddy choose words to draw and write on the lines. Read all the sentences together.

Draw and say.

1. A _____ is white.

2. A _____ is white.

3. A _____ is white.

4. A _____ is white.

5. _____ are white.

6. _____ are white.

7. _____ are white.

8. _____ are white.

LEARNING COLORS AND SHAPES ● Identifying colors and objects; hands-on activity; vocabulary development; reading sentences. Use *The Addison-Wesley Picture Dictionary*, picture books, and magazines. Be sure Buddy Tutor knows that first four nouns are to be singular, last four plural. Use of is/are, like *he/she*, is just something Learner must memorize, so don't worry if Learner mixes them up early on. Have Buddies write more sentences on a separate piece of paper if they need more practice.

Rainbow Mini-Book

Help your Buddy make a book like the one shown below. Fold 5 pieces of paper in half. Then make a cover. Staple the pages together when all the pages are illustrated and labeled. Read your book together.

Write and draw. Make a book.

A _____ is blue.   _____ are blue.

A _____ is red.   _____ are red.

A _____ is yellow.   _____ are yellow.

A _____ is green.   _____ are green.

A _____ is brown.   _____ are brown.

A _____ is black.   _____ are black.

A _____ is white.   _____ are white.

RAINBOW BOOK By _____

A leaf is green.

Trees are green.

LEARNING COLORS AND SHAPES ● Review of colors; review of *is/are*; hands-on activity; vocabulary development; writing sentences. Encourage Buddies to find new examples for each color; or, they may choose from items on pages 35-50. Place completed projects in class library. You may want to save of copy of this page in the Learner's **Assessment Portfolio.**

AMAZING WORDS

Help your Buddy write color names from the color pages you worked on. The words can be any ones your Buddy wants. One word goes in each square. Fill up the grid. Then take turns choosing squares. Read the words. Try to read 3 in a row correctly to get the bonus points. The player with the most points wins.

Write, say, and win!

3 in a row = 10 Bonus Points

Each square = 5 points

© Addison-Wesley Publishing Company

LEARNING COLORS AND SHAPES ● Playing a game; socializing; practicing word recognition. This game is played like Tic-Tac-Toe. Copy this page before it is filled in so that Buddies can play more than once. If you have more than one Buddy Learner in your class, they can exchange gameboards and play against one another. To make rules more challenging: each word in a sentence, name another word that begins (ends) with the same letter, etc. Buddies can "handicap" the Tutor with harder rules. Players can cover their squares with a coin or button.

Point to each shape. Say the names. Have your Buddy repeat.

Look, listen, and say.

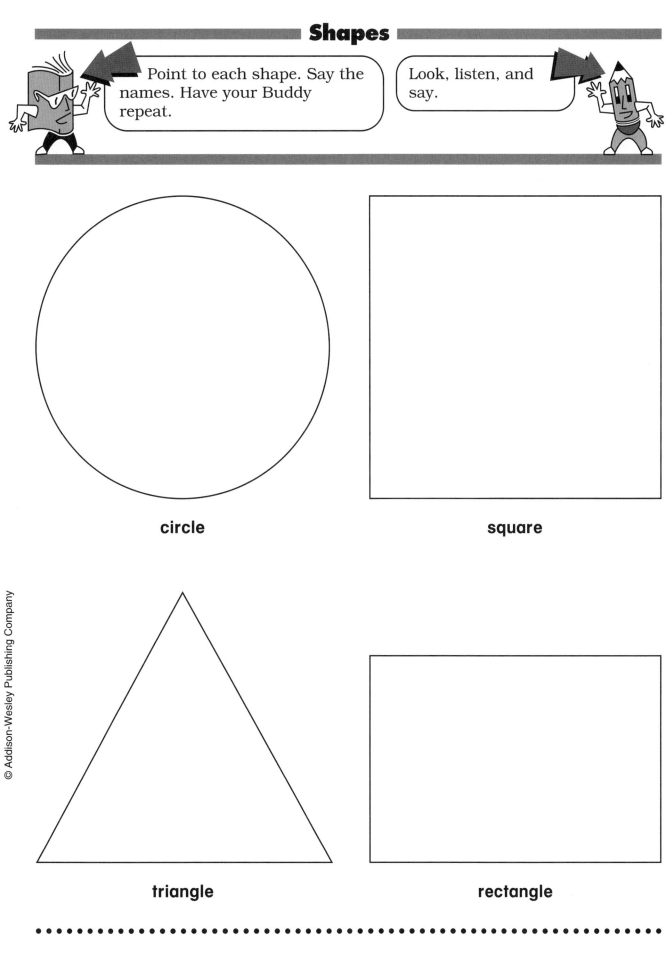

circle

square

triangle

rectangle

LEARNING COLORS AND SHAPES ● Identifying shapes; vocabulary development. Have Buddies review page 15 for more examples of shapes.

What Is a Circle?

After your Buddy draws pictures, help him or her label each picture, if necessary. Read all the sentences out loud. Your Buddy will repeat.

Draw, write, and read.

1. A __clock__ is a circle.

2. A _____ is a circle.

3. A _____ is a circle.

4. A _____ is a circle.

5. _____ are circles.

6. _____ are circles.

7. _____ are circles.

8. _____ are circles.

LEARNING COLORS AND SHAPES ● Identifying shapes and objects; hands-on activity; vocabulary development. Let Buddies look through *The Addison-Wesley Picture Dictionary* and books and magazines for vocabulary. Assist with labeling if necessary. Be sure Buddy Tutor knows that first four nouns are to be singular, last four plural.

After your Buddy draws pictures, help him or her label each picture, if necessary. Read all the sentences out loud. Your Buddy will repeat.

Draw, write, and read.

1. A _____window_____ is a square.

2. A _____ is a square.

3. A _____ is a square.

4. A _____ is a square.

5. _____ are squares.

6. _____ are squares.

7. _____ are squares.

8. _____ are squares.

LEARNING COLORS AND SHAPES ● Identifying shapes and objects; hands-on activity; vocabulary development. Let Buddies look through *The Addison-Wesley Picture Dictionary* and books and magazines for vocabulary. Assist with labeling if necessary. Be sure Buddy Tutor knows that first four nouns are to be singular, last four plural.

What Is a Triangle?

After your Buddy draws pictures, help him or her label each picture, if necessary. Read all the sentences out loud. Your Buddy will repeat.

Draw, write, and read.

1. A ___volcano___ is a triangle.

2. A _____ is a triangle.

3. A _____ is a triangle.

4. A _____ is a triangle.

5. _____ are triangles.

6. _____ are triangles.

7. _____ are triangles.

8. _____ are triangles.

LEARNING COLORS AND SHAPES ● Identifying shapes and objects; hands-on activity; vocabulary development. Let Buddies look through *The Addison-Wesley Picture Dictionary* and books and magazines for vocabulary. Assist with labeling if necessary. Be sure Buddy Tutor knows that first four nouns are to be singular, last four plural.

What Is a Rectangle?

After your Buddy draws pictures, help him or her label each picture, if necessary. Read all the sentences out loud. Your Buddy will repeat.

Draw, write, and read.

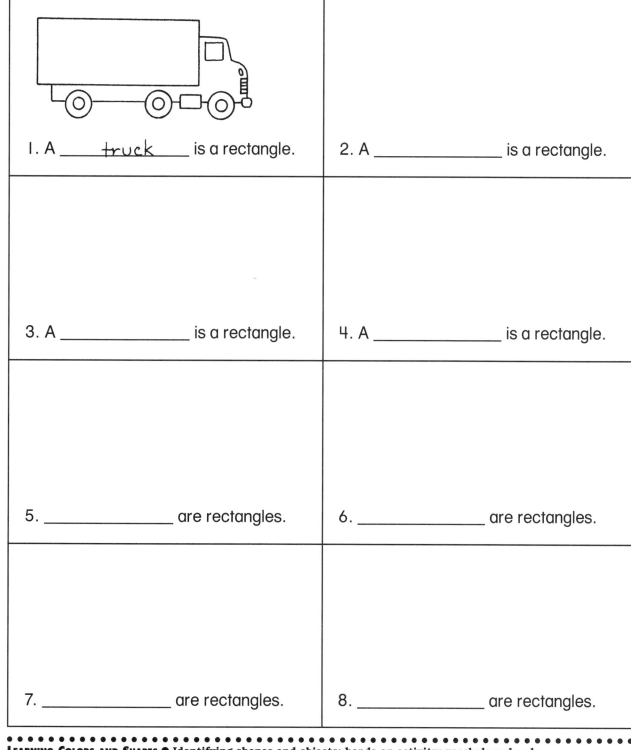

1. A _____truck_____ is a rectangle.

2. A _____ is a rectangle.

3. A _____ is a rectangle.

4. A _____ is a rectangle.

5. _____ are rectangles.

6. _____ are rectangles.

7. _____ are rectangles.

8. _____ are rectangles.

LEARNING COLORS AND SHAPES ● Identifying shapes and objects; hands-on activity; vocabulary development. Let Buddies look through *The Addison-Wesley Picture Dictionary* and books and magazines for vocabulary. Assist with labeling if necessary. Be sure Buddy Tutor knows that first four nouns are to be singular, last four plural.

Questions and Answers

Read all the questions out loud. Help your Buddy answer and fill in the blanks. Then have your Buddy ask **you** the questions.

Listen, say, read, and write.

1. *What's your name?*

   My name's _____.

2. *What's the name of your school?*

   It's _____.

3. *What grade are you in?*

   I'm in the _____ grade.

4. *What's your teacher's name?*

   My teacher's name is _____.

5. *What room are you in?*

   I'm in room _____.

6. *Where are you from?*

   I'm from _____.

7. *What's your address?*

   My address is_____.

8. *What's your phone number?*

   My phone number is _____.

QUESTIONS AND ANSWERS (REVIEW) ● **Asking for/giving personal information; vocabulary review; socializing; reading simple sentences.** Make two copies of this page, one for each Buddy. This page provides an opportunity for Buddies to review earlier vocabulary. If you have several Buddy Learners in class, pair them to ask and answer questions. You may want to give a mini-lesson on contractions with *is*. You may want to save a copy of this page in the Learner's **Assessment Portfolio.**

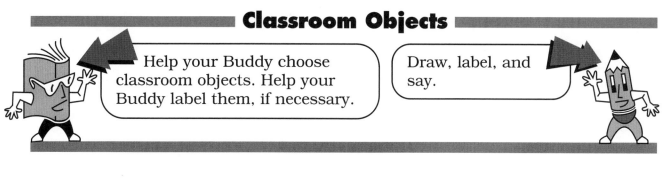

Classroom Objects

Help your Buddy choose classroom objects. Help your Buddy label them, if necessary.

Draw, label, and say.

pencil

IDENTIFYING/DESCRIBING OBJECTS, CLOTHES, AND PEOPLE ● Identifying and labeling objects; vocabulary development; hands-on activity. *The Addison-Wesley Picture Dictionary* will be useful for this activity (see page 55 of the dictionary).

59

BIG and LITTLE

Say each word on page 59 and describe it as "big" or "little." Help your Buddy choose eight words to draw and write in the blanks.

Listen, write, and read.

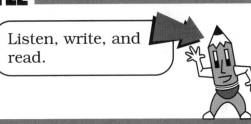

BIG	LITTLE
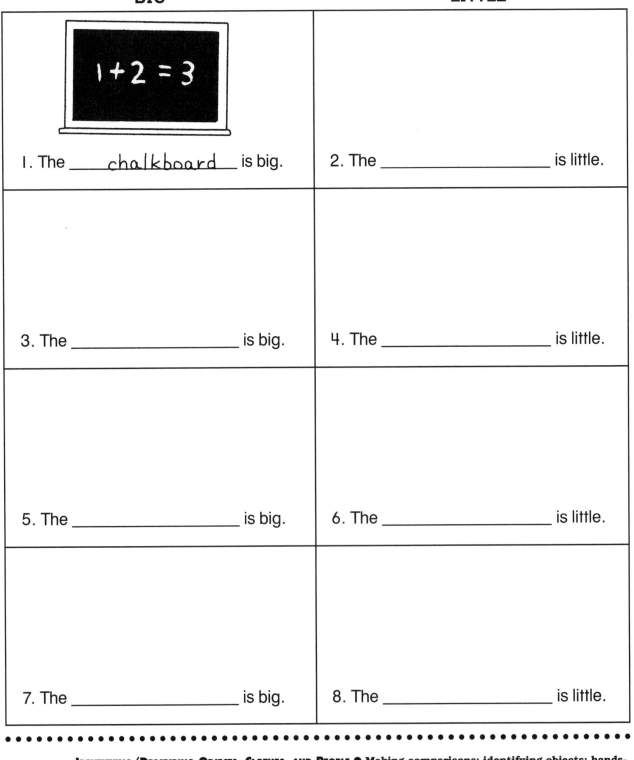 1. The __chalkboard__ is big.	2. The _____ is little.
3. The _____ is big.	4. The _____ is little.
5. The _____ is big.	6. The _____ is little.
7. The _____ is big.	8. The _____ is little.

IDENTIFYING/DESCRIBING OBJECTS, CLOTHES, AND PEOPLE ● Making comparisons; identifying objects; hands-on activity. Have Buddy Learner write more big/little sentences on a separate piece of paper if more practice is needed.

A. Shapes Cut out shapes of different sizes and colors for your Buddy to find. Make up more commands. Then let your Buddy give you some commands.

Listen and say.

1. Find a big, blue rectangle.
3. Find a big, yellow triangle.

2. Find a little, red square.
4. Find a little, green circle.

B. Classroom Objects
Gather some classroom objects. Hold up each object and ask your Buddy what it is. Let your Buddy ask you, too.

Listen and say.

Buddy Tutor: What's this?

Buddy Learner: It's a _____.

C. Classroom Commands
Ask your teacher for permission to play this game. Give your Buddy commands. Make up some new ones. Can your Buddy give **you** commands?

Listen, do, and say.

1. Go to the pencil sharpener.
3. Go to the teacher's desk.

2. Stand at the door.
4. Open your book.

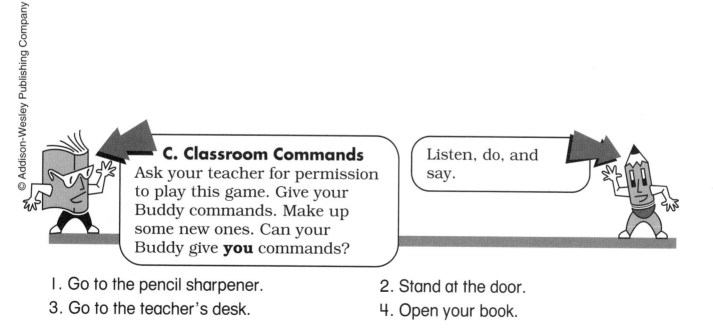

IDENTIFYING/DESCRIBING OBJECTS, CLOTHES, AND PEOPLE ● Identifying shapes and objects; following TPR directions; asking/answering questions; using the imperative. If possible, provide attribute shapes for students to use for Exercise A. Pairs of Buddy Learners can play games as well.

Challenge!

Read the sentences to your Buddy. Make up some more commands. Take turns telling each other what to draw.

Listen, draw, and say.

1. Draw a big, blue circle.

2. Draw a little, red pencil.

3. Draw a big, orange desk.

4. Draw a big, green chalkboard.

5. Draw a little, black book.

6. Draw a big, purple clock.

7. Draw a little, brown chair.

8. Draw a little, yellow door.

9. Draw a big, blue window.

10. Draw a little, orange rectangle.

11. Draw a big, black square.

12. Draw a little, green flag.

13. Draw a big, red calendar.

14. Draw a big, brown triangle.

15. Draw a little, yellow table.

IDENTIFYING/DESCRIBING OBJECTS, CLOTHES, AND PEOPLE ● Identifying colors, shapes, and objects; following directions; hands-on activity. Buddies can refer to *The Addison-Wesley Picture Dictionary* for more ideas. Pairs of Buddy Learners can play "Challenge" game. You may want to save a copy of this page in the Learner's **Assessment Portfolio.**

Help your Buddy choose clothes to draw and label. Ask your Buddy to say the names of the clothes.

Draw, write, and read.

pants

IDENTIFYING/DESCRIBING OBJECTS, CLOTHES, AND PEOPLE ● Identifying clothing; hands-on activity; reading words. Buddies can use the *The Addison-Wesley Picture Dictionary.* Page 35 will be especially useful.

What Are They Wearing?

Read the sentences with your Buddy. Help your Buddy to write the color words in the blanks.

Color the pictures. Read the sentences.

He's wearing a _____ hat.

He's wearing a _____ shirt.

He's wearing a _____ tie.

He's wearing a _____ jacket.

He's wearing _____ pants.

His belt is _____.

His socks are _____.

His shoes are _____.

This is a man.

This is a woman.

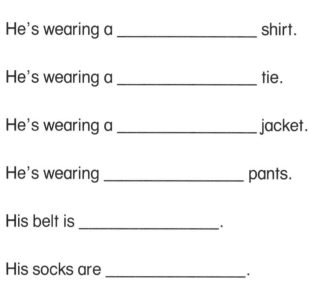

She's wearing a _____ blouse.

She's wearing a _____ sweater.

She's wearing a _____ skirt.

Her purse is _____.

Her raincoat is _____.

Her hat is _____.

Her earrings are _____.

IDENTIFYING/DESCRIBING OBJECTS, CLOTHES, AND PEOPLE ● Identifying colors and clothes; writing color words; vocabulary development; reading sentences; hands-on project. Provide crayons for Buddy Learner to color clothes of man and woman. Tutors can help Learners identify new articles of clothing in drawing of woman: *blouse, purse, raincoat.* Note two sentence patterns for the descriptions.

What Are You Wearing Today?

Draw yourself in the top box. Write about the clothes you are wearing. Read about it to your Buddy. Tell your Buddy to draw himself or herself in the bottom box and to write what he or she is wearing.

What are you wearing today? Read to your Buddy.

I'm a _____.
I'm wearing

_____.

_____.

_____.

_____.

_____.

I'm a _____.
I'm wearing

_____.

_____.

_____.

_____.

_____.

Now follow these directions.

1. Cut out a picture of a person from a clothes catalog.

2. Glue it on another piece of paper.

3. Write a description of the clothes.

© Addison-Wesley Publishing Company

IDENTIFYING/DESCRIBING OBJECTS, CLOTHES, AND PEOPLE ● Describing oneself; describing others; reviewing clothing and colors; art activity. Before describing their clothes, Buddies identify themselves as boys or girls. Provide clothing catalogs for second activity. Assist Buddies by giving example sentence patterns: *This is a woman. Her skirt is red*, etc.

Give your Buddy directions. "Color the jacket blue," "Color the hat red." Ask your Buddy to say which clothes he or she is putting on the boy and girl.

Color, cut, and say.

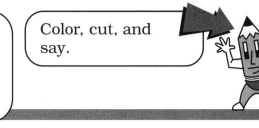

© Addison-Wesley Publishing Company

IDENTIFYING/DESCRIBING OBJECTS, CLOTHES, AND PEOPLE ● Following directions; hands-on activity; identifying colors and clothing. Buddies can use the models as paper dolls if they wish.

67

Give your Buddy directions. "Color the jacket blue," "Color the hat red." Ask your Buddy to say which clothes he or she is putting on the boy and girl.

Color, cut, and say.

68 **IDENTIFYING/DESCRIBING OBJECTS, CLOTHES, AND PEOPLE ● Following directions; hands-on activity; identifying colors and clothing.** Buddies can use the models as paper dolls if they wish.

A Clothes Mini-Book

Help your Buddy choose articles of clothing to make a book. Help your Buddy read and follow the directions.

Read, do, and write.

1. Choose two pictures for each sentence. Write two sentences for each page. Read all the sentences to your Buddy. For example, for sentence 1, find pictures of two pairs of pants.
2. Cut the pictures out.
3. Glue the pictures on a piece of white paper.
4. Write the sentence under each pair of pants. (This is for sentence 1.)
5. Now do the same for each kind of clothes. (Do this for sentences 2-18.)
6. Use one page for each kind of clothes.

1. The pants are_____.

2. The shirt is _____.

3. The sweater is _____.

4. The jacket is _____.

5. The shorts are _____.

6. The socks are _____.

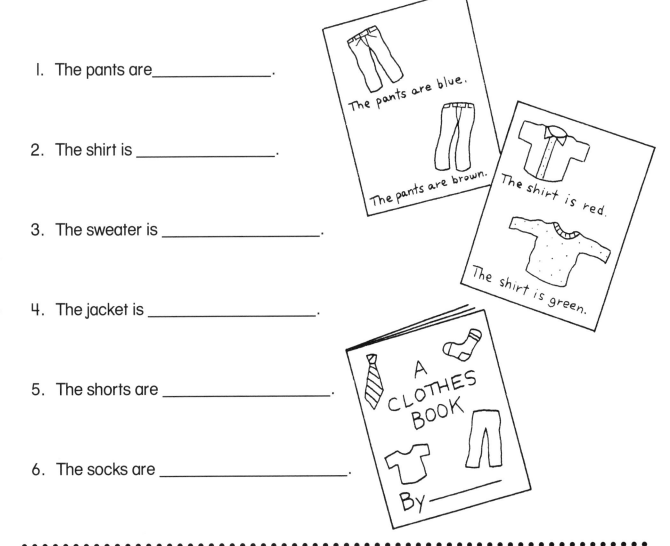

7. The shoes are _____.

8. The tie is _____.

9. The belt is _____.

10. The dress is _____.

11. The skirt is _____.

12. The hat is _____.

13. The underwear is _____.

14. The T-shirt is _____.

15. The bathrobe is _____.

16. The pajamas are_____.

17. The nightgown is _____.

18. The purse is _____.

IDENTIFYING/DESCRIBING OBJECTS, CLOTHES, AND PEOPLE ● Reading and following directions; identifying clothing; hands-on project; completing sentences. Provide mail-order catalogs and magazines for Buddies to cut up. Assist with book-making if necessary. Place completed projects in class library. Allow Learners to accept *pants* and *pajamas* as forms that just have to be memorized. You may want to save a copy of this project in the Learner's **Assessment Portfolio.**

AMAZING WORDS

Help your Buddy write clothes words from the clothes pages you worked on. The words can be any ones your Buddy wants. One word goes in each square. Fill up the grid. Then take turns choosing squares. Read the words. Try to read 3 in a row correctly to get the bonus points. The player with the most points wins.

Write, say, and win!

3 in a row = 10 Bonus Points

Each square = 5 points

IDENTIFYING/DESCRIBING OBJECTS, CLOTHES, AND PEOPLE ● Playing a game; socializing; practicing word recognition. This game is played like Tic-Tac-Toe. Copy this page before it is filled in so that Buddies can play more than once. If you have more than one Buddy Learner in your class, they can exchange gameboards and play against one another. To make rules more challenging: use each word in a sentence, name another word that begins (ends) with the same letter, etc. Buddies can "handicap" the Tutor with harder rules. Players can cover their squares with a coin or button.

Read each word. If necessary, help your Buddy draw lines to each part of the face. Then help your Buddy draw a person's head or cut a picture of a head from a magazine. Have your Buddy write the names of the parts of the face.

Listen, say, and draw lines. Then write.

forehead

nose

chin

eyes

cheeks

neck

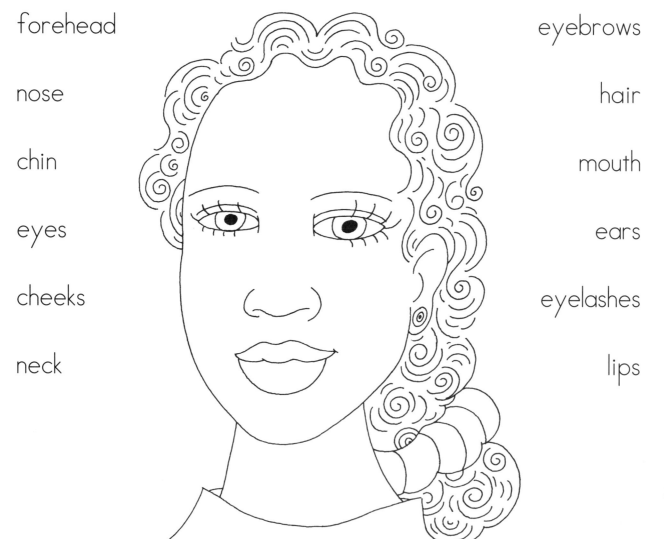

eyebrows

hair

mouth

ears

eyelashes

lips

IDENTIFYING/DESCRIBING OBJECTS, CLOTHES, AND PEOPLE ● Identifying body parts; following directions; writing. Remind Tutors not to give too much help—Learners are likely to know many body parts already. You may want to save a copy of this page in the Learner's **Assessment Portfolio.**

Parts of the Body 2

Read each word. If necessary, help your Buddy draw lines to each part of the body. Then help your Buddy draw a person or cut a picture of a person from a magazine. Have your Buddy write the names of the parts of the body.

Listen, say, and draw lines. Then write.

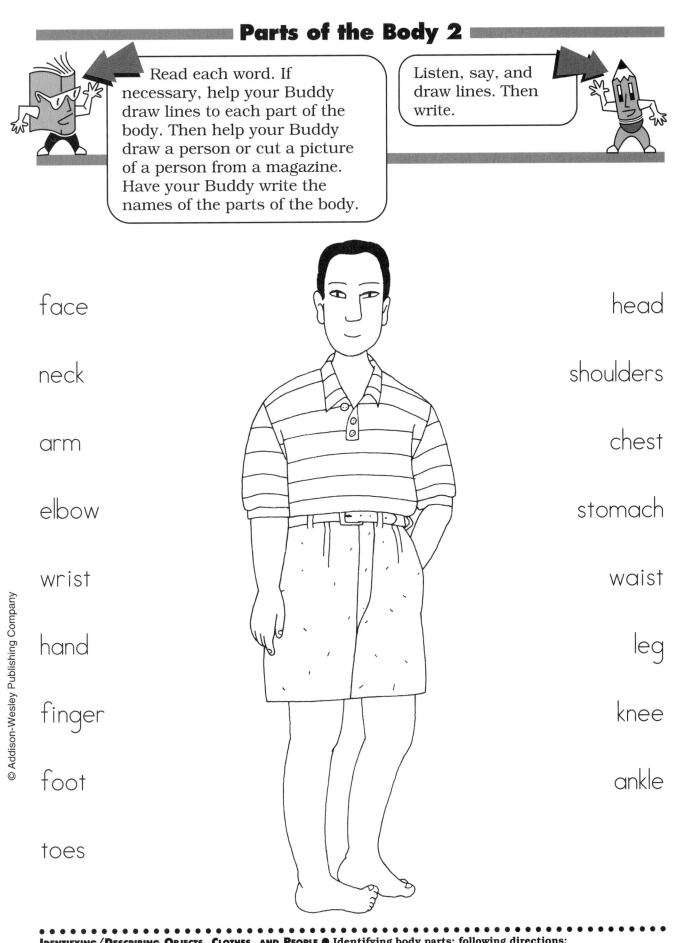

face

neck

arm

elbow

wrist

hand

finger

foot

toes

head

shoulders

chest

stomach

waist

leg

knee

ankle

IDENTIFYING/DESCRIBING OBJECTS, CLOTHES, AND PEOPLE ● Identifying body parts; following directions; writing. Remind Tutors not to give too much help—Learners are likely to know many body parts already. Buddies can draw people or cut pictures from magazines and label the facial and other body parts. You may want to save a copy of this page in the Learner's **Assessment Portfolio**.

73

Robot Body Parts

Read the sentences out loud before and after your Buddy completes them.

Read, write, and read again.

This robot's name is _____.

It has _____ heads.

It has _____ eyes.

It has _____ noses.

It has _____ mouths.

It has _____ arms.

It has _____ legs.

It has _____ feet.

It has _____ ears.

one	two	three	four	five	six	seven	eight	nine	ten

IDENTIFYING/DESCRIBING OBJECTS, CLOTHES, AND PEOPLE ● Completing sentences; reading; writing; enjoying creativity/fantasy. Extension: Have Buddy Learners use a separate piece of paper to draw a robot and write sentences about it. Encourage them to be as imaginative as possible. You may want to save a copy of this page in the Learner's **Assessment Portfolio.**

How Many?

Read the sentences out loud before and after your Buddy completes them.

Read, write, and read again.

I have _____ head. I have _____ nose. I have _____ eyes. I have

_____ ears. I have _____ mouth. I have _____ chin. I have

_____ arms. I have _____ elbows. I have _____ hands. I have

_____ fingers. I have _____ knees. I have _____ feet. I have

_____ toes.

Help your Buddy fill in the blanks and read the sentences.

Now write about a friend. Remember:
girl: **She** has
boy: **He** has

This is my friend _____. _____ has _____ head. _____

has _____ nose. _____ has _____ eyes. _____ has

_____ ears. _____ has _____ mouth.

My friend is wearing _____

_____

_____.

| one | two | three | four | five | six | seven | eight | nine | ten |

IDENTIFYING/DESCRIBING OBJECTS, CLOTHES, AND PEOPLE ● Learning numbers and body parts; describing people; reviewing clothing; reading and writing sentences. You may want to use this page for drilling other pronouns: *you have/we have/they have*. Buddies may wish to draw pictures or take photos of each other. You may want to save a copy of this page in the Learner's **Assessment Portfolio.**

How Are You?

See if your Buddy can read the body part words. Help if necessary. Then take turns acting out the conversation.

Read and say.

1. head

2. neck

3. arm

4. stomach

5. leg

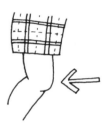

6. knee

7. chest

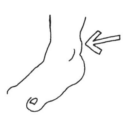

8. ankle

9. wrist

Hi. How are you?

Not so good.

What's the matter?

My _____ hurts.

· ·

IDENTIFYING/DESCRIBING OBJECTS, CLOTHES, AND PEOPLE ● Reviewing body parts; reading words; creating dialogues from cues. Encourage Buddies to extend conversation: "Did you fall down (have an accident, eat too much," etc.)?"

AMAZING WORDS

Help your Buddy write body parts words from the body parts pages you worked on. The words can be any ones your Buddy wants. One word goes in each square. Fill up the grid. Then take turns choosing squares. Read the words. Try to read 3 in a row correctly to get the bonus points. The player with the most points wins.

Write, say, and win!

3 in a row = 10 Bonus Points

Each square = 5 points

IDENTIFYING/DESCRIBING OBJECTS, CLOTHES, AND PEOPLE ● Playing a game; socializing; practicing word recognition. This game is played like Tic-Tac-Toe. Copy this page before it is filled in so that Buddies can play more than once. If you have more than one Buddy Learner in your class, they can exchange gameboards and play against one another. To make rules more challenging: use each word in a sentence, name another word that begins (ends) with the same letter, etc. Buddies can "handicap" the Tutor with harder rules. Players can cover their squares with a coin or button.

Describing People

Read the words with your Buddy. Then help him or her find magazine pictures of people who match each word. Glue the pictures on a piece of white paper, and help your Buddy write the words under the pictures.

Read the words, find pictures, and write.

fat   thin   tall   short   average

old   young   curly hair   straight hair

long hair   short hair   dark hair   light hair

IDENTIFYING/DESCRIBING OBJECTS, CLOTHES, AND PEOPLE ● Describing people; vocabulary development; matching words to pictures; following directions. Encourage Tutors to get Learners started and then to let them work independently. Extension: Have Buddies cut out magazine pictures of lots of human and animal heads and bodies. They can paste them together in strange ways (a dog's head on a duck's body, e.g.) and name the "new creatures" they've created.

Me and My Buddy

Help your Buddy choose correct words to describe you both. Read all the sentences out loud.

Listen, read, and write.

ME

I am _____ years old.

I am _____ and _____.

My eyes are _____.

My hair is _____ and

_____.

ME

I am _____ years old.

I am _____ and _____.

My eyes are _____.

My hair is _____ and

_____.

MY BUDDY

_____ is _____

years old. _____ is _____

and _____.

_____ eyes are _____.

_____ hair is _____

and _____.

MY BUDDY

_____ is _____

years old. _____ is _____

and _____.

_____ eyes are _____.

_____ hair is _____

and _____.

IDENTIFYING/DESCRIBING OBJECTS, CLOTHES, AND PEOPLE ● Describing people; making comparisons.
Students will of course complete charts twice, once describing themselves, once describing their Buddy. If they want to, Buddies can draw each other.You may want to save a copy of this page in the Learner's
Assessment Portfolio.

Help your Buddy choose foods to draw. If necessary, help your Buddy label them. Talk about what color they are as you say the words: "Apples are red."

Draw, write, and say.

apples

TALKING ABOUT FOOD AND FAMILY ● Identifying foods; writing; vocabulary development; art project. Have Buddies use *The Addison-Wesley Picture Dictionary* (page 51 is especially useful) and food magazines for ideas. Extension: Have Buddy Learner draw five special foods from his or her country.

Help your Buddy choose foods from page 80. Read all the sentences out loud with your Buddy. Help your Buddy write the names of the foods in the blanks. Say, "I do, too" when it's a food you like.

Draw pictures of foods you like to eat. Read the sentences.

1. I like _____.

2. I like _____.

3. I like _____.

4. I like _____.

5. I like _____.

6. I like _____.

7. I like _____.

8. I like _____.

TALKING ABOUT FOOD AND FAMILY ● Discussing food choices; writing; reading sentences; art project.
Buddies may need help using count/noncount nouns; e.g., *I like apples; I like pie.*

I Don't Like ....

Help your Buddy choose foods from page 80. Read all the sentences out loud with your Buddy. Help your buddy write the names of the foods in the blanks. Say, "I don't, either" when it's a food you don't like.

Draw pictures of foods you don't like to eat. Read the sentences.

1. I don't like _____.

2. I don't like _____.

3. I don't like _____.

4. I don't like _____.

5. I don't like _____.

6. I don't like _____.

7. I don't like _____.

8. I don't like _____.

TALKING ABOUT FOOD AND FAMILY ● Discussing food choices; writing; reading sentences; art project.
Buddies may need help using count/noncount nouns; e.g., *I don't like apples; I don't like pie.*

What's for Lunch?

Help your Buddy pack a lunch. Ask, "Do you like rice?" Help your Buddy to circle foods he or she likes and to cross out foods he or she doesn't like.

What do you like for lunch?

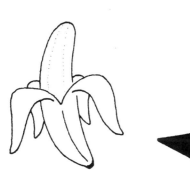

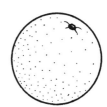

TALKING ABOUT FOOD AND FAMILY ● **Stating food preferences; matching words to pictures; home-school connection.** Instruct Tutor to have Learner say "Yes, I like ___" for circled foods and "No, I don't like ___" for for the crossed out foods. Extension: Buddies can pack real lunches together and have a picnic, indoors or outdoors, at school or home.

Help your Buddy take a survey of your class and fill in the chart. The students will write in their own names. Your Buddy will write in the names of the foods. Help your Buddy ask each time, "What do you like?" and "What don't you like?"

Ask questions and write.

NAME	LIKES	DOESN'T LIKE
1.		
2.		
3.		
4.		
5.		
6.		
7.		
8.		
9.		
10.		

TALKING ABOUT FOOD AND FAMILY ● Taking a survey; filling in a chart; making comparisons; discussing preferences. Extension: You may wish to extend this page into a graphing activity. List foods down the side of a graph with numbers of students across the top. Have the Buddy Learners help you count students' votes and fill in appropriate blocks on the graph. You can also have the Buddy Learners write sentences using this information: *Corey likes pizza, but he doesn't like hot dogs.*

Meals

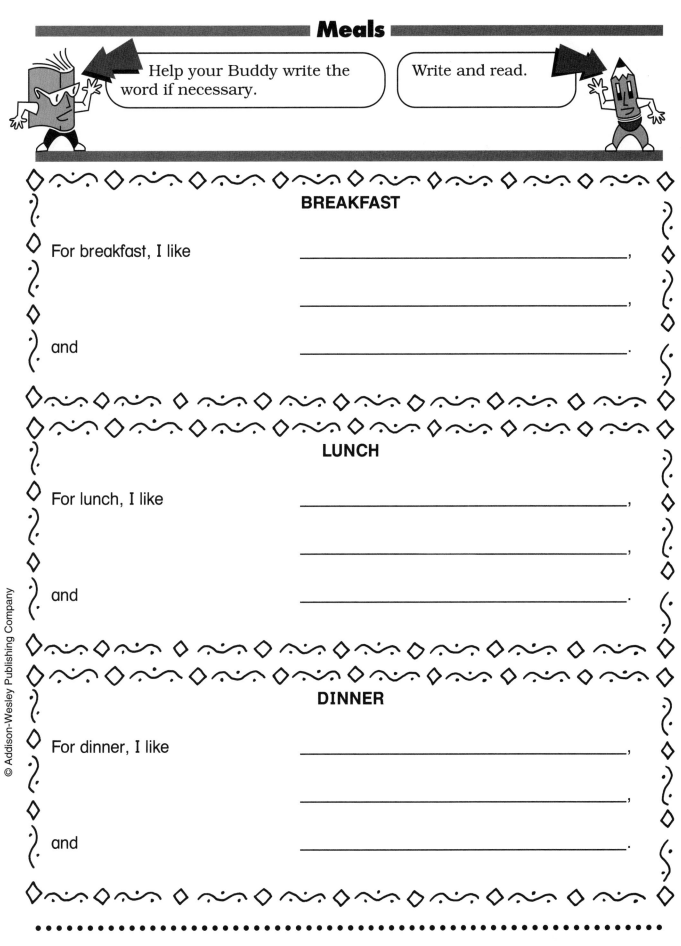

Help your Buddy write the word if necessary.

Write and read.

BREAKFAST

For breakfast, I like

_____,

_____,

and _____.

LUNCH

For lunch, I like

_____,

_____,

and _____.

DINNER

For dinner, I like

_____,

_____,

and _____.

TALKING ABOUT FOOD AND FAMILY ● Guided sentence writing; stating food preferences; reading sentences. Buddies can discuss their favorite meals with each other and classmates. Extension: Buddies can create and decorate a menu, plan and make a meal together, invite other students, and/or host a class party.

85

Food Mini-Book

Help your Buddy choose food items to make a book. Have your Buddy write one sentence on each page of the book. He or she can draw or cut out pictures for each page.

Fill in the sentences. Read each sentence to your Buddy. Then make a book.

I like _____, but I don't like

_____.

I like _____, but I don't like

_____.

I like _____, but I don't like

_____.

I like _____, but I don't like

_____.

I like _____, but I don't like

_____.

I like _____, but I don't like

_____.

FOOD BOOK

By _____

I like apples, but I don't like onions.

TALKING ABOUT FOOD AND FAMILY ● Stating food preferences; hands-on/art project; reading compound sentences. Six sentences are listed here, but of course Buddies can make bigger books if they choose. Assist with mechanics if necessary. Place completed project in class library. You may want to save a copy of this project in the Learner's **Assessment Portfolio.**

Help your Buddy write food words from the food pages you worked on. The words can be any ones your Buddy wants. One word goes in each square. Fill up the grid. Then take turns choosing squares. Read the words. Try to read 3 in a row correctly to get the bonus points. The player with the most points wins.

Write, say, and win!

3 in a row = 10 Bonus Points

Each square = 5 points

© Addison-Wesley Publishing Company

TALKING ABOUT FOOD AND FAMILY ● Playing a game; socializing; practicing word recognition. This game is played like Tic-Tac-Toe. Copy this page before it is filled in so that Buddies can play more than once. If you have more than one Buddy Learner in your class, they can exchange gameboards and play against one another. To make rules more challenging: use each word in a sentence, name another word that begins (ends) with the same letter, etc. Buddies can "handicap" the Tutor with harder rules. Players can cover their squares with a coin or button.

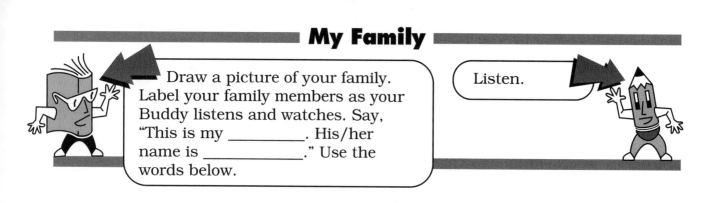

Draw a picture of your family. Label your family members as your Buddy listens and watches. Say, "This is my _____. His/her name is _____." Use the words below.

Listen.

Now watch and help your Buddy draw a picture of his/her family. Then help your Buddy describe the family. Use the words below.

Draw, write, and say.

| Grandmother | Mother | Sister | Aunt | Cousin |
| Grandfather | Father | Brother | Uncle | Cousin |

TALKING ABOUT FOOD AND FAMILY ● Home-school connection; listening comprehension; describing family members. Allow time for Buddy pairs to share their family pictures. Discuss some of the information with the entire class, to model sentences such as *Tran has two sisters. Their names are _____ and _____. His mother's name is _____,* etc. Buddies may need to use extra paper for their drawings. Have Learners take this page home to share with their families.

Family Clothes Mini-Book

Make a Family Clothes Book.
Follow these directions for the father,
for sentence 1. Repeat for all the
family members. Make a cover for
your book. Staple the pages together.
1. Choose a piece of colored paper.
2. Cut out a shirt for the father.
3. Glue it on a piece of white paper.
4. Draw the rest of the father.
5. Write the sentence under it.
6. Use one page for each picture.

Make a Family
Clothes Book.

1. This is the father. He's wearing a _____ shirt.

2. This is the mother. She's wearing a _____ dress.

3. This is the brother. He's wearing _____ pants.

4. This is the sister. She's wearing a _____ sweater.

5. This is the baby. She's wearing _____ pajamas.

6. This is the aunt. She's wearing a _____ skirt.

7. This is the uncle. He's wearing a _____ jacket.

8. This is the grandmother. She's wearing a _____ blouse.

9. This is the grandfather. He's wearing a _____ hat.

10. These are the cousins. They're wearing _____ shoes and

_____ socks.

FAMILY
CLOTHES
BOOK

BY _____

TALKING ABOUT FOOD AND FAMILY ● Home-school connection; hands-on project; reviewing colors, clothing, and family members; guided sentence writing. Assist Buddies with project as necessary. Be sure they
understand that the clothing items they are to cut out of colored paper must correspond to items in sentences
1-10 (shirt, dress, pants, etc.). Remind students how to staple book together. Have Learners take this project
home to share with their families.

Make a Family Food Book. Use the sentences below to write about each person in your family. Draw pictures. Make a cover. Staple it all together.

Make a Family Food Book.

This is my _____. (mother / sister / aunt / grandmother / cousin)

She likes _____, but she doesn't like _____.

This is my _____. (father / brother / uncle / grandfather / cousin)

He likes _____, but he doesn't like _____.

FAMILY FOOD BOOK

By _____

This is my brother. He likes spaghetti,

but he doesn't like hot dogs.

© Addison-Wesley Publishing Company

TALKING ABOUT FOOD AND FAMILY ● Home-school connection; hands-on project; reviewing food preferences; taking a survey; using affirmative and negative constructions; using 3rd person inflections; **writing compound sentences.** Encourage Learners to make a page for every family member. You may also make this a chart or graph activity. You may want to save a copy of this project in the Learner's **Assessment Portfolio.** Have Learners take this project home to share with their families.

At Home: Where Does It Go?

Help your Buddy label the objects on this page. Have your Buddy repeat the words. Then have him/her cut them out and glue them in the correct rooms on page 92.

Look, say, and write.

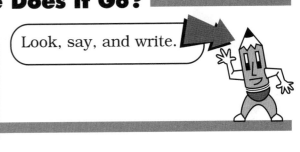

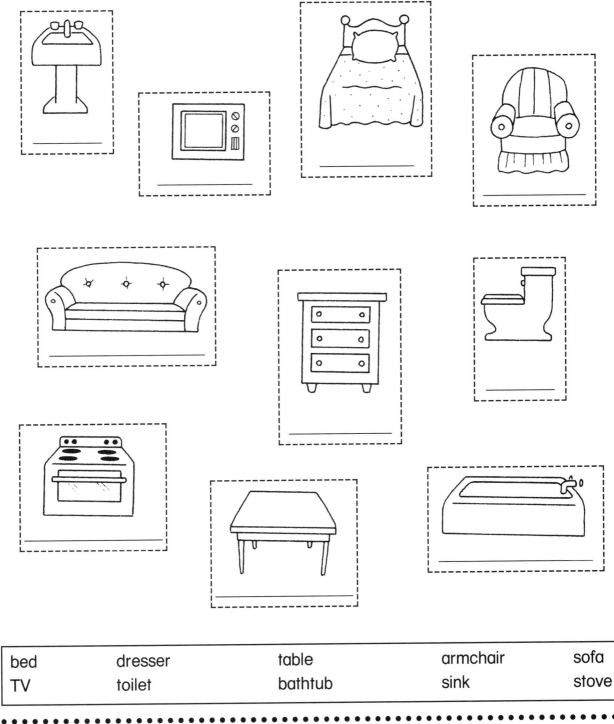

bed	dresser	table	armchair	sofa
TV	toilet	bathtub	sink	stove

© Addison-Wesley Publishing Company

DESCRIBING LOCATIONS AND ACTIONS ● Identifying household objects/furniture; hands-on activity; vocabulary development; home-school connection. Buddies use boxed words for labeling objects. Encourage Buddy tutors to help Learners draw and label more objects to place in the room. You may want to help Learner understand appropriate use of words such as *bathroom, rest room, toilet,* etc. Have Learners take this project home to share with their families.

In the House

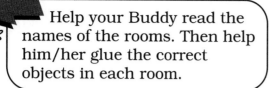

Help your Buddy read the names of the rooms. Then help him/her glue the correct objects in each room.

Read, listen, and glue.

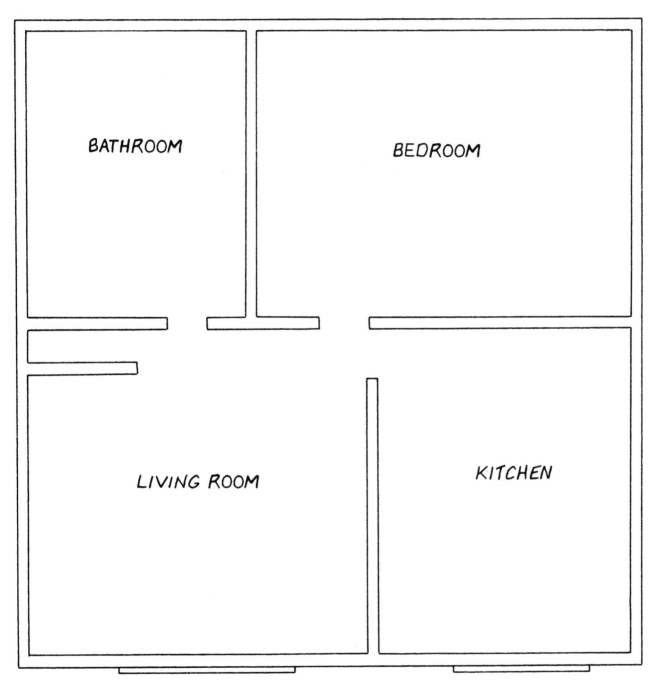

BATHROOM

BEDROOM

LIVING ROOM

KITCHEN

DESCRIBING LOCATIONS AND ACTIONS ● Identifying household objects/furniture; identifying rooms in a house; hands-on activity; vocabulary development; home-school connection. Have Learners take this project home to share with their families.

What Are They Doing?

Help your Buddy choose activities for each room. Then have your Buddy fill in each blank and draw a picture to go with it.

Read, write, and draw.

She's in the living room.

She's *reading*.

She's in the bedroom.

She's _____.

He's in the kitchen.

He's _____.

She's in the kitchen.

She's _____.

He's in the living room.

He's _____.

He's in the bathroom.

He's _____.

Actions

washing dishes	watching TV	making dinner
sleeping	doing homework	getting dressed
sweeping the floor	reading	talking on the phone
eating breakfast		

• •

DESCRIBING LOCATIONS AND ACTIONS ● Reviewing rooms in a house; using present progressive verb tense.
Have Buddies make up dialogues based on page: "Where is she? She's in the living room. What is she doing?
She's reading," etc. You may want to save a copy of this page in the Learner's **Assessment Portfolio**.

A Neighborhood

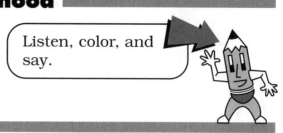

Give your Buddy directions for coloring the words in the pictures. For example, "Color the houses blue," or "Color the buses yellow." Then make up sentences for your Buddy to repeat: "There are nine houses," "There is one police car," etc.

Listen, color, and say.

house

police car

school

post office

school bus

fire station

church

apartment building

grocery store

playground

laundromat

drug store

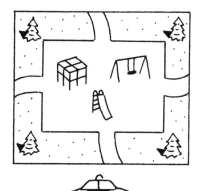

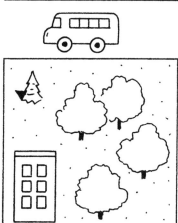

DESCRIBING LOCATIONS AND ACTIONS ● Home-school connection; identifying places in a neighborhood/town; following directions; practicing *There is/are.*; practicing *s/es* plural endings. Use *The Addison-Wesley Picture Dictionary* for more ideas for places Buddies can draw in their "town." Have students take these pages home to share with their families.

AMAZING WORDS

Help your Buddy write object and place words from previous pages. The words can be any ones your Buddy wants. One word goes in each square. Fill up the grid. Then take turns choosing squares. Read the words. Try to read 3 in a row correctly to get the bonus points. The player with the most points wins.

Write, say, and win!

3 in a row = 10 Bonus Points

Each square = 5 points

© Addison-Wesley Publishing Company

DESCRIBING LOCATIONS AND ACTIONS ● Playing a game; socializing; practicing word recognition. This game is played like Tic-Tac-Toe. Copy this page before it is filled in so that Buddies can play more than once. If you have more than one Buddy Learner in your class, they can exchange gameboards and play against one another. To make rules more challenging: use each word in a sentence, name another word that begins (ends) with the same letter, etc. Buddies can "handicap" the Tutor with harder rules. Players can cover their squares with a coin or button.

Street Smarts

Help your Buddy read these safety tips.

Read the sentences out loud.

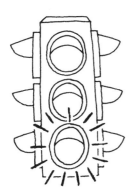

1. Green means "go."
   Cross on green.

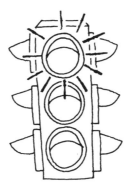

2. Red means "no."
   Stop on red.

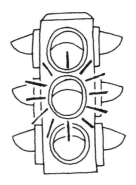

3. Yellow means "be careful."
   Do not cross on yellow.

4. Look both ways.

5. Press the pedestrian button.

6. Walk in the crosswalk.

7. Listen to the crossing guard.

8. Listen to the bus driver.

9. Wear your seat belt in the car.

DESCRIBING LOCATIONS AND ACTIONS ● Following directions; learning about safety; reading; home-school connection. If appropriate, you can make this a combined TPR activity and field trip: Have Buddies take a walk to practice safety tips 1-6. Send students to an interesting destination, such as a museum or the public library, if they are nearby.

Help your Buddy read the list below. Then help him or her write the things and people that belong in each room.

Read and write.

LIBRARY

BATHROOMS

CAFETERIA

OFFICE

CLASSROOM

books	sink	secretary	computer
lunch tray	tables	chairs	backpacks
bookcase	desks	telephone	chalkboards
toilets	clocks	teachers	students
principal			

© Addison-Wesley Publishing Company

DESCRIBING LOCATIONS AND ACTIONS ● Identifying/reviewing people and objects; reading; practicing
Where is/are **and** *It's/They're/She's/He's*; **asking/answering questions.** Buddies can make up dialogues:
"Where's the secretary? She's in the office. Where are the students? They're in the classroom," etc.

On the Playground

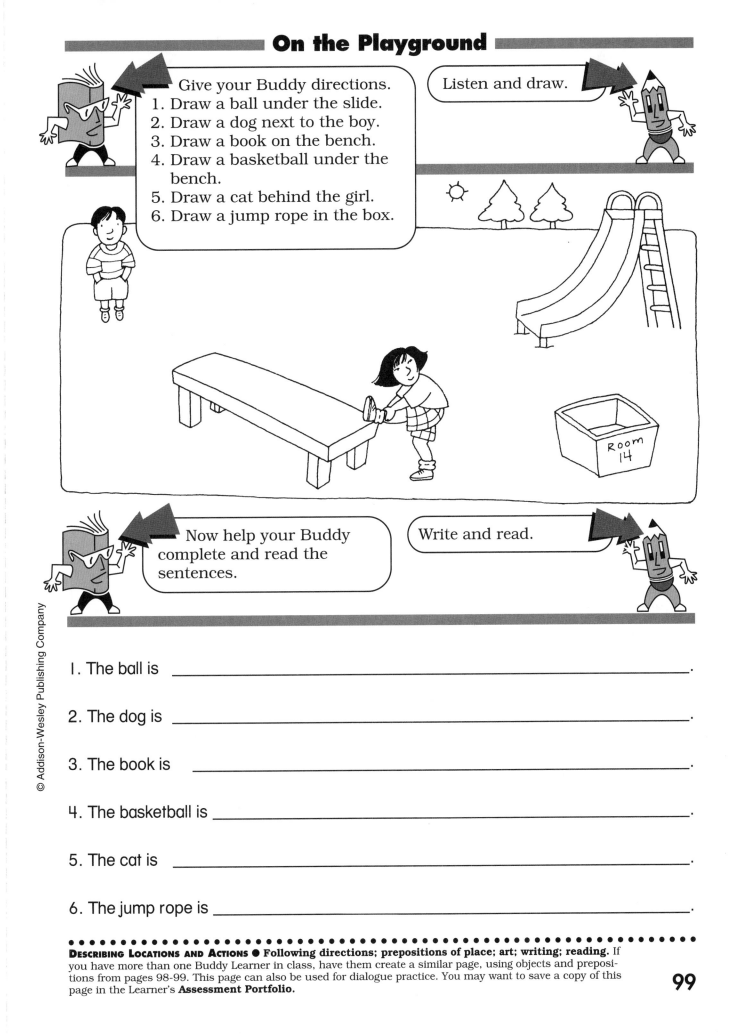

Give your Buddy directions.
1. Draw a ball under the slide.
2. Draw a dog next to the boy.
3. Draw a book on the bench.
4. Draw a basketball under the bench.
5. Draw a cat behind the girl.
6. Draw a jump rope in the box.

Listen and draw.

Room 14

Now help your Buddy complete and read the sentences.

Write and read.

1. The ball is _____.

2. The dog is _____.

3. The book is _____.

4. The basketball is _____.

5. The cat is _____.

6. The jump rope is _____.

© Addison-Wesley Publishing Company

DESCRIBING LOCATIONS AND ACTIONS ● Following directions; prepositions of place; art; writing; reading. If you have more than one Buddy Learner in class, have them create a similar page, using objects and prepositions from pages 98-99. This page can also be used for dialogue practice. You may want to save a copy of this page in the Learner's **Assessment Portfolio.**

Where Are They? What Are They Doing?

Help your Buddy choose words from the "where" list for the first sentence, and from the "what" list for the second one.

Look, say, and write.

She's _in the bathroom_ .

She's _washing her hands_ .

She's _____ .

She's _____ .

She's _____ .

She's _____ .

He's _____ .

He's _____ .

He's _____ .

He's _____ .

He's _____ .

He's _____ .

Where	
in the cafeteria	in the office
in the bathroom	on the playground
in the library	in the classroom

What	
kicking a soccer ball	eating lunch
singing	studying
talking on the phone	washing her hands

DESCRIBING LOCATIONS AND ACTIONS ● Prepositions of place; reviewing locations; practicing present progressive verb tense; asking and answering questions; practicing dialogues. Buddies can make up dialogues based on page: "Where is she? She's in the bathroom. What is she doing? She's washing her hands," etc. You may want to save a copy of this page in the Learner's **Assessment Portfolio.**

100

What Are You Doing?

Have your Buddy choose words from the list at the bottom of the page and fill in the blanks.

Write, read, and draw pictures.

What are you doing?	What are you doing?
I'm _____smiling_____.	I'm _____.
What are you doing?	**What are you doing?**
I'm _____.	I'm _____.
What are you doing?	**What are you doing?**
I'm _____.	I'm _____.

eating	laughing	running	jumping rope
doing my homework	singing	playing kickball	playing the piano
washing dishes	cooking	sweeping the floor	swimming

© Addison-Wesley Publishing Company

DESCRIBING LOCATIONS AND ACTIONS ● Present progressive verb tense with and without objects; art; reading; writing; practicing dialogues. After Buddies complete page, have them use sentences for dialogue practice. Other Buddy Learners in class can join in.

What Are They Doing?

Help your Buddy choose words from the list at the bottom of the page and fill in the blanks.

Write, read, and draw pictures.

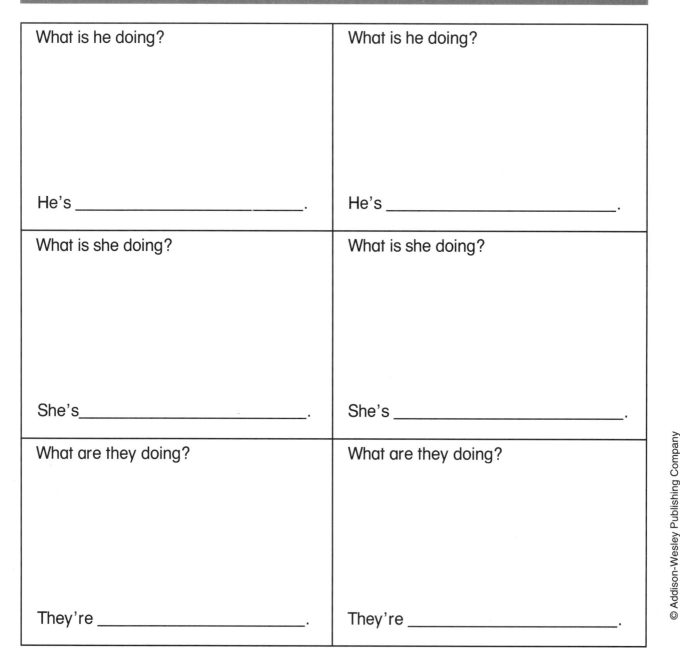

What is he doing?

He's _____.

What is he doing?

He's _____.

What is she doing?

She's _____.

What is she doing?

She's _____.

What are they doing?

They're _____.

What are they doing?

They're _____.

eating	laughing	running	jumping rope	doing homework
singing	playing kickball	playing the piano	washing dishes	cooking
swimming	sweeping the floor	riding a bike		

DESCRIBING LOCATIONS AND ACTIONS ● Present progressive verb tense with and without objects; art; reading; writing; practicing dialogues. After Buddies complete page, have them use sentences for dialogue practice. Other Buddy Learners in class can join in. Be sure Buddy Tutors monitor Learner's pronouns.

Act It Out Game

Follow these directions.
1. Cut out the squares on this page and on the next page.
2. Put the squares into a bag or jar.
3. Take turns picking squares and acting out the activity on it.
4. Guess what your Buddy is doing.
5. Play with other friends.

fly	jump	play jump rope	run
walk	climb	sit down	stand up
laugh	smile	listen to music	ride a bike
swim	eat	play baseball	play soccer

dance

sing

play the piano

play guitar

cry

talk on the phone

wash dishes

cook

do my homework

sleep

wake up

read

write

do karate

play kickball

play tennis

© Addison-Wesley Publishing Company

DESCRIBING LOCATIONS AND ACTIONS ● Action verbs; verbs with objects; TPR activity; pantomiming; hands-on activity; playing a game; socializing. Involve all Buddy Learners, as well as other in class, in game. After students play the game using *I'm (doing my homework)*, have them play again, using other pronouns: *She's doing her homework*, etc.

104

Help your Buddy use the words from pages 103-104 to write sentences. Then he or she can draw pictures.

Read, write, and draw.

I can _swim_____.

I can _____.

I can _____.

I can _____.

I can _____.

I can _____.

I can _____.

I can _____.

DESCRIBING ABILITIES AND SCHEDULES ● Modal *can*; action verbs; verbs with objects; art; writing; reading.
Buddy Learners can write more sentences about what they <u>can</u> do on a separate piece of paper.

Help your Buddy use the words from pages 103-104 to write sentences. Then he or she can draw pictures.

Read, write, and draw.

I can't play the guitar .

I can't _____.

I can't _____.

I can't _____.

I can't _____.

I can't _____.

I can't _____.

I can't _____.

DESCRIBING ABILITIES AND SCHEDULES ● Modal *can't*; action verbs; verbs with objects; art; writing; reading.
Buddy Learners can write more sentences about what they <u>can't</u> do on a separate piece of paper. Encourage Buddies to use verbs listed on pages 103-104 that pertain to <u>ability</u> ("I can't play the piano," "I can't fly a plane/drive a car," e.g.) rather than to circumstance or mood ("I can't talk on the phone," "I can't smile," etc.).

106

Take a Survey!

Find 5 girls and 5 boys in the class. Ask them what they can do. Then ask them what they can't do. Use this chart to record the information.

Ask questions and write.

GIRLS

Name	Can	Can't
1.		
2.		
3.		
4.		
5.		

BOYS

Name	Can	Can't
1.		
2.		
3.		
4.		
5.		

DESCRIBING ABILITIES AND SCHEDULES ● **Taking a survey; using a chart to record information; asking questions; socializing.** Extensions: Have Buddy Learners use a separate piece of paper to make up sentences about each student surveyed ("Jasmine can swim, but she can't fly a plane"). You may want to have students use information to make a comparison chart showing activities most/least reported; some Buddies may be ready to make a bar graph from the information on the chart.

School Schedule

Time		Activity
8:30 A.M.		Language Arts
9:30 A.M.		Recess
9:40 A.M.		Science
10:40 A.M.		Recess
10:50 A.M.		Math
12:15 P.M.		Lunch/recess
1:05 P.M.		Social Studies
2:20 P.M.		P.E.
2:55 P.M.		School ends

© Addison-Wesley Publishing Company

DESCRIBING ABILITIES AND SCHEDULES ● Telling time; reading a chart; talking about schedules and activities; asking and answering questions. If necessary, teach "At 8:30 Ho Yi has Language Arts," etc. to get Buddies started. You may need to preview the page with some practice in telling time. Buddy Learners can use page for dialogue practice: "What class does Ho Yi have at 9:40 every day?" "What time does Ho Yi eat lunch?" etc.

Our School Schedule

Work with your Buddy to make your school schedule.

Make a schedule.

	Time	Activity

DESCRIBING ABILITIES AND SCHEDULES ● Telling time; filling in a chart; talking about activities and schedules; asking and answering questions. If Buddy Tutor and Buddy Learner have different school schedules, have them make a copy of this page so they can each make a schedule; or, Buddy Tutor can just help Learner to make his or her schedule. Be sure Buddies draw clock hands in to correspond with times listed. Extension: Buddy Learners can use the page for dialogue practice ("What class do you have at 2:15?" "What time do you eat lunch?" etc.).

109

Daily Schedule

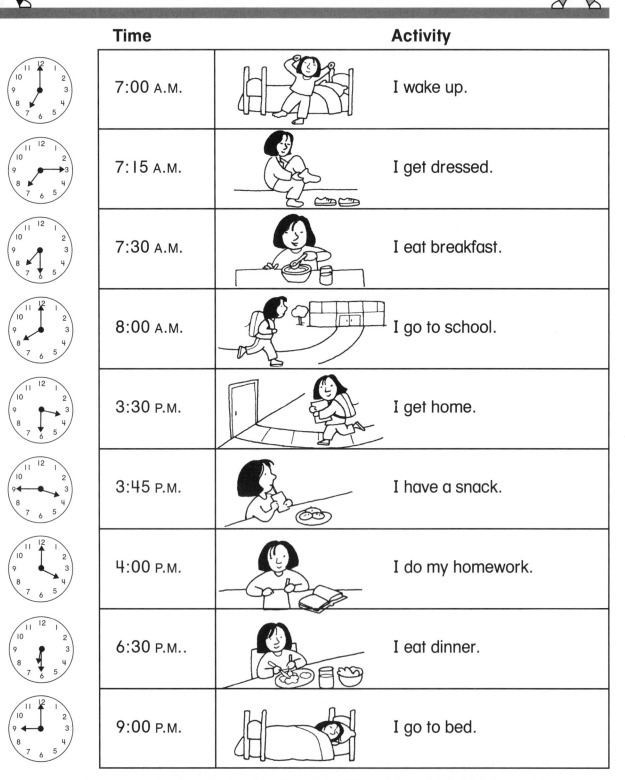

Time		Activity
7:00 A.M.		I wake up.
7:15 A.M.		I get dressed.
7:30 A.M.		I eat breakfast.
8:00 A.M.		I go to school.
3:30 P.M.		I get home.
3:45 P.M.		I have a snack.
4:00 P.M.		I do my homework.
6:30 P.M..		I eat dinner.
9:00 P.M.		I go to bed.

© Addison-Wesley Publishing Company

DESCRIBING ABILITIES AND SCHEDULES ● Home-school connection; telling time; reading a chart; talking about schedules and activities; asking and answering questions; practicing 3rd. person present tense verb endings. Buddy Learners can use page for dialogue practice: "What time does Saad get up every day?" "He gets up at 7:00," etc. Have Learners take this page home to share with their families.

Our Daily Schedules

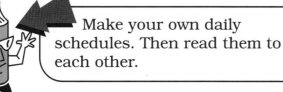

Make your own daily schedules. Then read them to each other.

Make a schedule.

Time	Activity

DESCRIBING ABILITIES AND SCHEDULES ● Telling time; filling in a chart; talking about activities and schedules; asking and answering questions. Have Buddies copy page so each can make his or her own daily schedule. Get their reading started by modeling, "I get up at 7:00 every day," etc. Have Buddy Learners practice dialogues based on page: "What time do you get up every day?" "I get up at 7:00 every day," etc. Extend for 3rd. person practice: "What time does Tran get up every day? He gets up at 7:00."

This

BUDDY BOOK

was made by

_____
name

from

_____
country

These buddies helped: _____

_____

_____

_____
Teacher

_____
School

_____
Date